THE VOICE OF FOOTBALL

SHOOT

KT-495-468

OUR ENGLAND. OUR TIME.

WE'RE SINGING FOR ENGLAND

ANNUAL EDITOR: Dan Tyler & Sam Horscraft
CONTRIBUTORS: Alfie House, Daniel Defalco, Oscar Johnson,
Patrick Austen-Hardy

/TheVoiceOfFootball   WWW.SHOOT.CO.UK   @_shootfootball

CONTENTS

06 YOUR PROFILE

07 BUILD YOUR CLUB

08 NAME THAT PLAYER

10 EXCLUSIVE: REECE & LAUREN JAMES

12 BROTHERS IN ARMS

14 GUESS THAT GROUND

16 SPOT THE BALL

18 THE AGE GAME

20 SOUTHGATE'S SHOES

22 EXCLUSIVE: NICK POPE

24 PREMIER LEAGUE SHARP SHOOTERS

26 SPOT THE STARS

28 KLOPP'S KOP KINGS

30 SALAH, FIRMINO OR MANE?

32 SUPER QUIZ - 1ST HALF

34 FAMOUS FANS

36 SUPER STOPPERS

38 NEW KIDS ON THE BLOCK

40 EXCLUSIVE: LUCY BRONZE

43 KIT SWAP

44 EXCLUSIVE: ELLEN WHITE

47 READY TO ROAR

48 EXCLUSIVE: MASON MOUNT

51 BLUE IS THE FUTURE

52 EXCLUSIVE: SCOTT MCTOMINAY

54 EXCLUSIVE: LEWIS MORGAN

56 BIG MONEY BUYS

58 EXCLUSIVE: TOM OGDEN

60 GUESS THE GAFFER

62 EXCLUSIVE: HARVEY BARNES

65 FIND THE FULL-BACK

66 TARGET TEN

68 SUPER QUIZ - 2ND HALF

70 BELIEVE IT OR NOT

72 CAPTION THIS

74 ADDED TIME

76 ANSWERS

THIS⁺
ANNUAL
BELONGS TO

NAME:

Jesse

AGE:

8

FAVOURITE TEAM:

Tottenham

FAVOURITE PLAYER:

Heung-Min Son

TEAM I PLAY FOR:

Teddington NPL

POSITION I PLAY:

Right Winger

PROFILE PICTURE:

BUILD YOUR CLUB

Create a new team to join the Shoot Super League!

CLUB NAME: Spaggelli Fc

STADIUM NAME: The Spagdiod

NICKNAME: The Spagetittd

CLUB BADGE

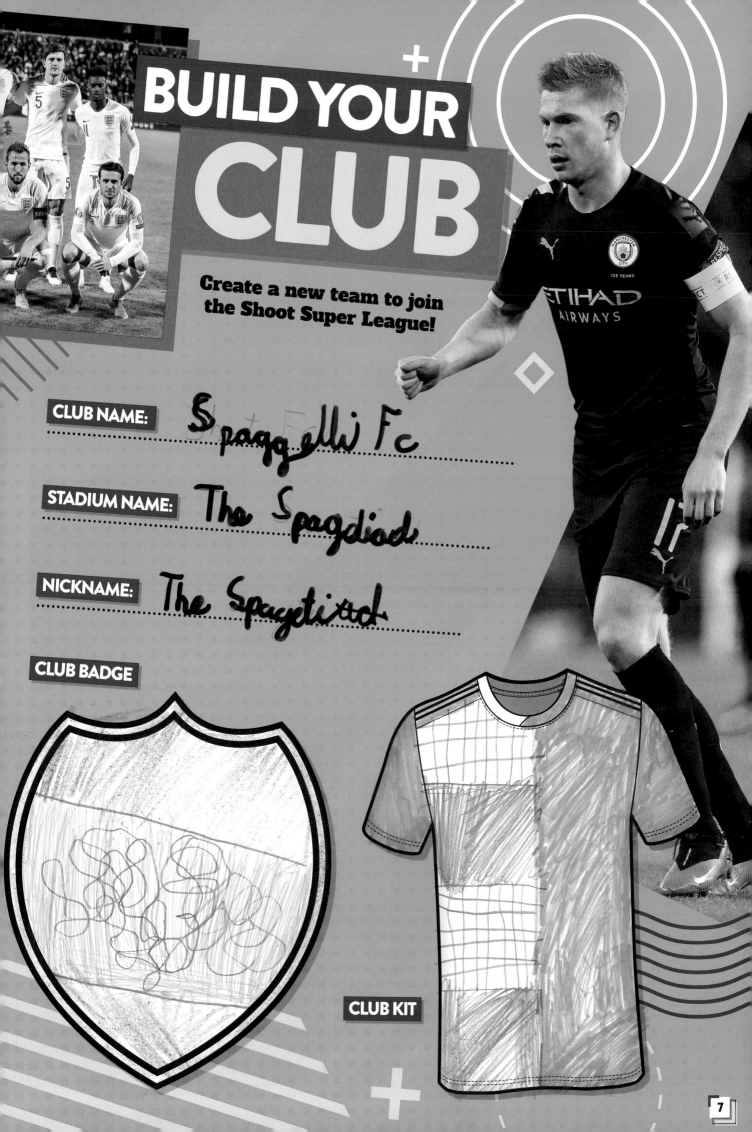

CLUB KIT

NAME THAT PLAYER

Can you reveal the full name of these 10 Premier League stars?

1 · variant chalk panto

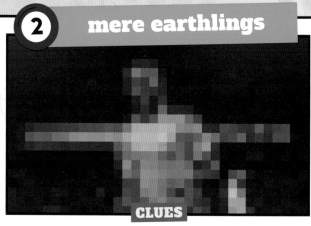

CLUES

- A full-back who loves to attack.
- Plays international football for the Netherlands.

Van Ahrolt

2 · mere earthlings

CLUES

- Two-time Premier League winner.
- England 2018 World Cup ace.

Raheim Sterling

3 · routine rain dog

CLUES

- Plays for a London club.
- International for Germany.

Antonio Rudeiger

4 · no bartender rows

CLUES

- Full-back with lots of assists.
- Captains his country.

Andrew Robertson

5 ice rider

CLUES
- Can play in defence or midfield.
- Scored England's winning penalty against Colombia at the 2018 World Cup.

eric dier

6 litany marathon

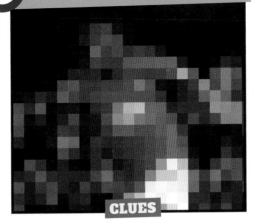

CLUES
- Moved to England from France.
- Wears the number 9 shirt for his club.

Anthony Martial

7 tattoo welch

CLUES
- Has played for three current Premier League teams.
- Went to the World Cup as a 16-year-old.

Theo Walcott

8 open special

CLUES
- A record signing for his club.
- Likes to play as a wide attacker.

Nicolas Pepe

9 donned hartman

CLUES
- Born in Birmingham.
- Has played for England at seven different age groups.

Nathan Redmond

10 she ran by sale

CLUES
- Has played in the top-five divisions in England.
- Moved to the Clarets from the Seagulls in 2014.

Ashley Barnes

Use the clubs to help you solve the anagrams.

ANSWERS ON PAGE 76

FACT FILE
LAUREN JAMES

POSITION: MIDFIELDER
HEIGHT: 1.75M (5FT 9IN)
DATE OF BIRTH: SEPTEMBER 29, 2001
PLACE OF BIRTH: KENNINGTON

FACT FILE
REECE JAMES

POSITION: RIGHT-BACK
HEIGHT: 1.82M (6FT 0IN)
DATE OF BIRTH: DECEMBER 8, 1999
PLACE OF BIRTH: KENNINGTON

THE JAMES'

Reece and Lauren James are living out the ultimate dream. Reece is playing for his boyhood club Chelsea, while younger sister Lauren is starring for Manchester United in the Women's Super League.

The talented siblings spoke to Shoot about growing up together, their dad's influence and what it's like to represent massive clubs at the top level.

What are your earliest footballing memories?

Lauren: "We just used to play football, football, football! There was a park out the back of our house and we'd always be over there. It's always been a passion of ours from a young age and now we're living it."

Reece: "There was a park just over the back of our house and we just used to be out there all day, every day playing with friends and other kids. When I wasn't playing with Chelsea, I was either playing there or training with my dad. I played whenever I could."

Has having a football loving family helped you?

Lauren: "I have always loved the game and that is probably because of my family. It was great growing up with my brothers (Josh and Reece) who loved to play football. I always wanted to play like them and with them. It was always football in our house."

Reece: "Josh loved to play and I looked up to him. I was playing with him and other older mates so I got used to the physical side. I learned a lot off him and then Lauren learned that off me. This probably helped us improve quicker than other kids."

Your dad is a UEFA licensed football coach and runs a coaching school (Nigel James Elite Coaching). How has he helped you in your career so far?

Lauren: "He's played a big part. As he's a coach he has helped us with our football. He made sure we got the basics right and that we were comfortable on the ball. He's always been there for us when we've needed his help. I'm very grateful for that."

Reece: "He's helped us a lot. When we were growing up we did a lot of sessions with him to get us to a level. He would go through technical drills which improved me quickly. He has taken a lot of time and effort to help us get to the level we're at."

Who was your footballing hero?

Lauren: "Luka Modric. As I play midfield I always used to watch him because he is such a good and clever player. I liked watching him and feel I could learn from his game."

Reece: "Didier Drogba. I used to play striker because I liked scoring a lot of goals. Drogba was one of the best in the world and was playing at the club I supported. I always looked up to him growing up."

How does it feel to be playing football at the top level?

Lauren: "It's a great feeling to play at the top level. It's always been a dream of mine since I was young to play at the top of the game but there's still a long way to go. I want to compete in the Champions League and play at World Cups with England. That's where I want to get to."

Reece: "It's great playing at one of the best leagues in the world and at one of the biggest clubs in the world. It's been a dream coming through and getting to show everyone what I can do at the club I've always supported."

You both play for very former successful players in Frank Lampard and Casey Stoney. How much help have they provided?

Lauren: "Casey has helped me a lot both on and off the pitch. She understands me as a person, a player and that has helped me grow. Because she's played at the highest level she has experienced many situations so is able to give me a lot of advice."

Reece: "He's been excellent for me. We all listen to everything Frank has to say because he's played at the highest level. His appointment has really helped us younger players come through and get opportunities. He has helped me improve my game, kept me focus and ready to perform."

You've both represented England at youth level so you must have ambitions of playing for the national side?

Lauren: "It's a dream and an ambition of mine to play for the England senior side. Hopefully as I progress, and keep doing well for my club, I'll end up getting a call-up. It would be exciting to do that, especially with the exposure the team have after the last two World Cups."

Reece: "Every footballer wants to play at the highest level and represent their country. It's everyone's dream to put on their country's shirt and I'm no different. If I'm doing it on the pitch for my club then I know I'll get a chance. The Euros getting pushed back a year helps me but I will need to be playing consistently next season to break into a very good squad."

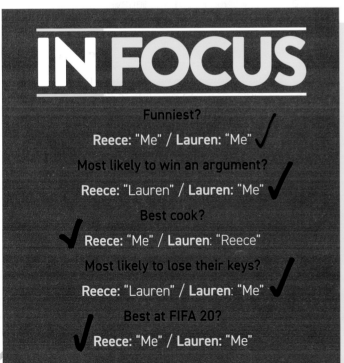

IN FOCUS

Funniest?

Reece: "Me" / **Lauren:** "Me" ✓

Most likely to win an argument?

Reece: "Lauren" / **Lauren:** "Me" ✓

Best cook?

✓ **Reece:** "Me" / **Lauren:** "Reece"

Most likely to lose their keys?

Reece: "Lauren" / **Lauren:** "Me" ✓

Best at FIFA 20?

✓ **Reece:** "Me" / **Lauren:** "Me"

BROTHERS

IN >>>>>>>

ARMS

Reece and Lauren James are not the only siblings to make it as professional footballers. There are actually quite a few dotted around the world. To get you started, here are seven talented sets of brothers currently playing the beautiful game...

HAZARD

Thorgan and Eden Hazard are both tricky wide players and Belgium internationals. Thorgan is currently impressing at Borussia Dortmund while older brother Eden is still settling at Real Madrid. Their younger sibling Kylian is a midfielder for Cercle Brugge.

POGBA

The Pogba brothers are a trio of professional footballers. Paul is a World Cup winner and superstar midfielder at Manchester United. Meanwhile, his older twin brothers Florentin and Mathias play as a defender and forward for Sochaux and Lorca.

ALCANTARA

Rafinha and Thiago both started their careers as midfielders at Barcelona. Their father Mazinho played football and won the 1994 World Cup with Brazil. Rafinha also plays for Brazil but brother Thiago, who is now at Bayern Munich, represents Spain.

XHAKA

The Xhakas are both combative midfield players at their respective clubs. Granit patrols the middle of the park for Arsenal and Switzerland while older brother Taulant plays for Basel and Albania. The pair played against each other in the opening match of Euro 2016 with Granit's Switzerland winning 1-0.

@tx.34

BOATENG

The Boatengs are half-brothers who wear the shirts of two different countries. Jerome is a defender who has won countless trophies with Bayern Munich and the World Cup with Germany. Meanwhile, midfielder, Kevin-Prince, has played for various clubs and represented Ghana at two World Cups.

@princeboateng

KROOS

The Kroos' are both midfielders with a real eye for a pass. Toni played a key part in helping Germany win the World Cup in 2014 and has won numerous trophies with Real Madrid. Younger brother Felix has played Bundesliga football with Werder Bremen and Union Berlin.

HERNANDEZ

Both Lucas and Theo Hernandez started their careers with their father's former team, Atletico Madrid. Lucas won a couple of trophies with the Spanish side and the World Cup with France before joining Bayern Munich. Younger brother Theo switched to rivals Real Madrid and is now playing for AC Milan.

GUESS THAT GROUND

Football stadiums come in all different sizes and designs. Can you match up the 10 pictures with the correct name? Use the capacity of each ground as a clue.

1 Capacity: 18,439

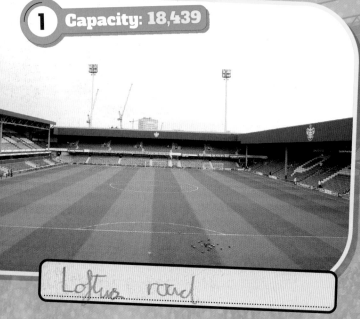

Loftus road

2 Capacity: 37,890

Elland Road

3 Capacity: 52,354

St James Park

4 Capacity: 42,785

Villa Park

5 Capacity: 55,017

Etihad STadium

6 Capacity: 31,367

Ewood Park

7 Capacity: 54,074

Anfield

8 Capacity: 20,620

Fratton Park

9 Capacity: 62,303

Tottenham Hotspur STadium

10 Capacity: 49,000

STadium Of Light

STADIUM NAMES

LOFTUS ROAD QPR	**FRATTON PARK** Portsmouth	**ST JAMES' PARK** Newcastle United
ETIHAD STADIUM Manchester City	**VILLA PARK** Aston Villa	**ANFIELD** Liverpool	**STADIUM OF LIGHT** Sunderland
ELLAND ROAD Leeds United	**EWOOD PARK** Blackburn Rovers	**TOTTENHAM HOTSPUR STADIUM** Tottenham Hotspur

SPOT THE BALL

There are six footballs in these four action photos. Can you guess which ball is the real one? Write your answers in the spaces below

GAME 1

CRYSTAL PALACE V NEWCASTLE UNITED

GAME 2

BRIGHTON AND HOVE ALBION WOMEN V BIRMINGHAM CITY WOMEN

16

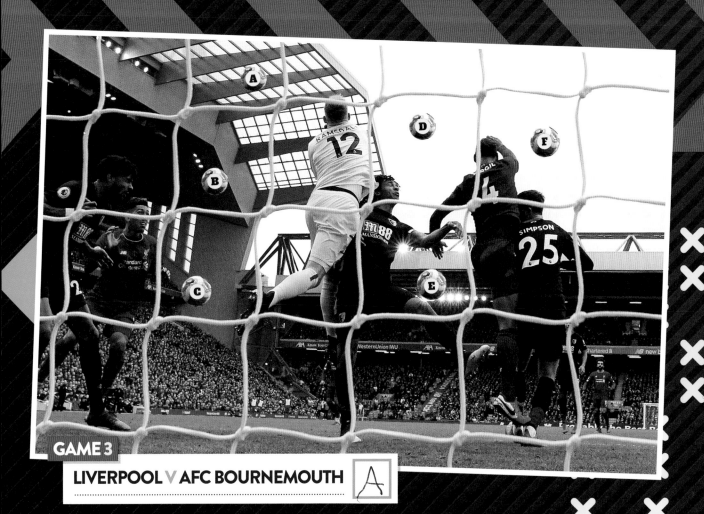

GAME 3

LIVERPOOL V AFC BOURNEMOUTH

GAME 4

MANCHESTER CITY WOMEN V ARSENAL WOMEN

ANSWERS ON PAGE 76

THE AGE GAME

Here are 10 superstar footballers but when were they born?. Can you match up each player with their correct birth year?

LIONEL MESSI

1987

CRISTIANO RONALDO

1985

JACK GREALISH

1995

SON HEUNG-MIN

1992

18

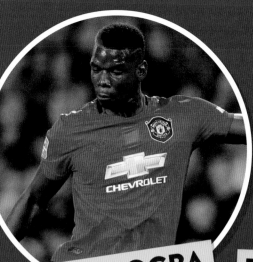

PAUL POGBA

_1993_

ZLATAN IBRAHIMOVIC

_1981_

BILLY GILMOUR

_2001_

KYLIAN MBAPPE

_1998_

EDEN HAZARD

_1991_

ALPHONSO DAVIES

_2000_

BORN IN

1981

BORN IN

2001

BORN IN

1998

BORN IN

1995

BORN IN

1993

BORN IN

1985

ANSWERS ON PAGE 76

SOUTHGATE'S SHOES

It's time to pick your England squad for next summer's European Championship.

We've given you the job of England manager. Your task is to step into Gareth Southgate's shoes and pick your 23 player squad for the European Championship. There are lots of options so use the roster to help. The nation awaits your decision. Good luck!

My England Squad

1. GK Jordan Pickford
2. DF Kyle Walker
3. DF Trent Alexander-Arnold
4. MF James Maddison
5. DF Reece James
6. DF Kieran Trippier
7. MF Jack Grealish
8. MF James Ward-Prowse
9. FW Raheem Sterling
10. FW Dominic Calvert-Lewin
11. FW Jadon Sancho
12. DF Harry Maguire

13. GK Nick Pope
14. FW Harry Kane
15. DF Ben Chilwell
16. DF Danny Rose
17. DF Tyrone Mings
18. DF/MF Aaron Wan-Bissaka
19. FW Danny Ings
20. MF Declan Rice
21. MF Harry Winks
22. MF/FW Marcus Rashford
23. GK Dean Henderson

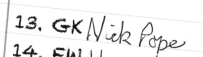

GOALKEEPERS

Jordan Pickford

Nick Pope

Dean Henderson

Tom Heaton

Ben Foster

Jack Butland

MIDFIELDERS

Jordan Henderson

Alex Oxlade-Chamberlain

Phil Foden

James Maddison

Dele Alli

Ruben Loftus-Cheek

Mason Mount

Jack Grealish

Ross Barkley

Fabian Delph

Eric Dier

Declan Rice

Harry Winks

Jesse Lingard

James Ward-Prowse

Bukayo Saka

DEFENDERS

Kyle Walker

Trent Alexander-Arnold

Kieran Trippier

Aaron Wan-Bissaka

Reece James

Danny Rose

Ben Chilwell

Luke Shaw

Joe Gomez

Harry Maguire

John Stones

Fikayo Tomori

Tyrone Mings

James Tarkowski

Michael Keane

Mason Holgate

FORWARDS

Raheem Sterling

Dominic Calvert-Lewin

Jadon Sancho

Marcus Rashford

Callum Hudson-Odoi

Harry Kane

Harvey Barnes

Tammy Abraham

Callum Wilson

Danny Ings

Mason Greenwood

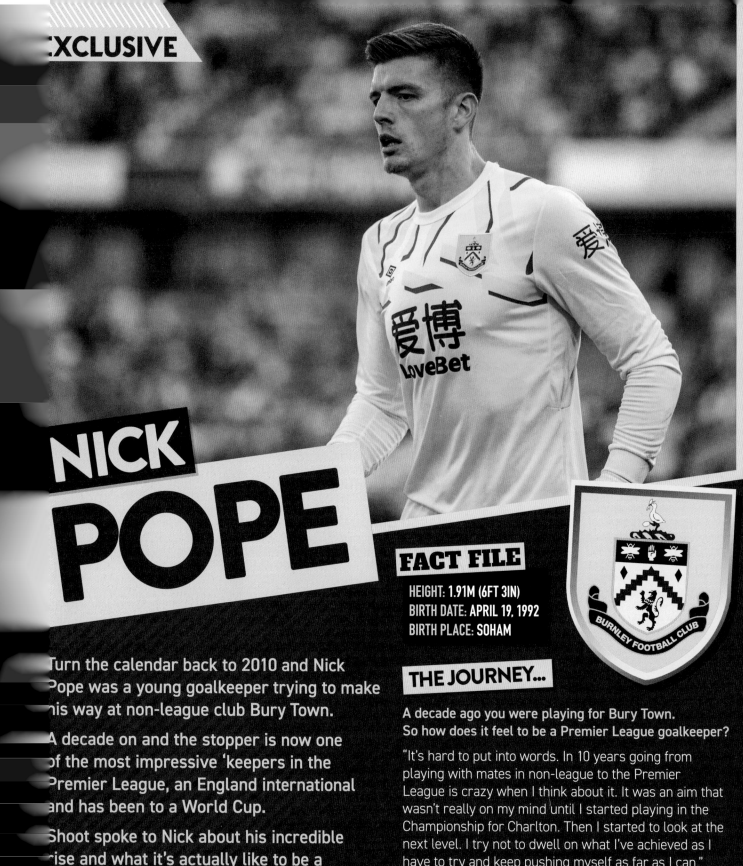

NICK
POPE

FACT FILE

HEIGHT: **1.91M (6FT 3IN)**
BIRTH DATE: **APRIL 19, 1992**
BIRTH PLACE: **SOHAM**

Turn the calendar back to 2010 and Nick Pope was a young goalkeeper trying to make his way at non-league club Bury Town.

A decade on and the stopper is now one of the most impressive 'keepers in the Premier League, an England international and has been to a World Cup.

Shoot spoke to Nick about his incredible rise and what it's actually like to be a top-level goalkeeper.

THE JOURNEY...

A decade ago you were playing for Bury Town. So how does it feel to be a Premier League goalkeeper?

"It's hard to put into words. In 10 years going from playing with mates in non-league to the Premier League is crazy when I think about it. It was an aim that wasn't really on my mind until I started playing in the Championship for Charlton. Then I started to look at the next level. I try not to dwell on what I've achieved as I have to try and keep pushing myself as far as I can."

What was it like to be part of England's 2018 World Cup squad after having a brilliant breakthrough Premier League season?

"To make my Premier League debut, help Burnley finish seventh, make my England debut and then go to the World Cup was an unbelievable season. To be part of the squad to go to Russia and to see all the support for us back home was great. We're proud to have reached the semi-final but there will always be that feeling that we felt we could've gone that one step further."

GOALKEEPING...

You've played at many different levels of the game but what's the main difference from a goalkeeper's point of view?

"You actually get more touches the lower you go down the leagues. This is because the games can be a bit more end to end and a lot more high balls will be put into the box. In the Premier League there's more build up play and when the ball comes into the box it is usually a low cross or passing move. The sharpness in the Premier League is the most noticeable difference. Things happen quickly so I have to be concentrated and ready so that I make the right decisions when needed."

What's the worst thing about being a goalkeeper?

"If the team get battered then everyone takes a look at the goalkeeper even if there's not a lot you can do about the goals. It's also harder for us to correct an error compared to an outfield player who has an opportunity to score a goal. Another tough thing about being a goalkeeper is that you get moaned at a lot!"

Do you feel it's even more important to be able to play with your feet now than it was when you started your career?

"There has been a real development to that side of being a goalkeeper and it's definitely something that I've noticed is more important the higher the level I've played. More and different things are expected of us now than there ever has been. For the teams in the Premier League who like to build from the back, being a goalkeeper is not just about saving shots."

All goalkeepers are good at saving shots but what do you think works for you?

"I just try and stay on my feet as long as I possibly can. It's important not to gamble and go to ground too early because it makes it easier for the attacker. If I can stay on my feet then they will have to beat me. I have pride in trying to keep the ball out of the net and I just try to not give the attacker anything. If I do then I know they will punish me, especially in the Premier League."

What's it like to face shots in the Premier League and at international level?

"In the Premier League it is different and shots are coming in at top level speed. It was a steep learning curve when I first started experiencing that but it's something that I've got more and more used to. Training with Burnley a year before making my league debut really helped as I was facing shot after shot from top level players every single day in training."

When the ball is down the other end, how do you keep yourself mentally switched on?

"Over the years I've actually learnt when to switch off a little bit. When I first started playing in the Championship I think I would try and concentrate too much. That might sound funny but I'd actually end up being mentally fatigued which can lead to mistakes. So now I'm a lot better at switching on and off when I need to in a game. This helps keep me mentally fresh and ready for when the team needs me."

What would you say you need to be a top goalkeeper?

"Try to improve the things you aren't good at and keep improving what you are good at. Don't be afraid to try new things in training and take them into a game if they work for you. Be confident by viewing a match as a stage to perform your skills on and show people what you've got. Also it's important to try and stay positive even if you make a mistake. All goalkeepers make errors but it's how you recover that's important."

IN FOCUS

Goalkeeping Heroes:
Richard Wright and Petr Cech

Most played artist on your playlist: George Ezra

One save you could watch on repeat:
High to my left vs Josh Sims
(Southampton) in 2018

First car: 1.1 litre red Citroen C2

Hardest striker to read: Harry Kane

PREMIER LEAGUE SHARP SHOOTERS

A host of world-class strikers have lit up the Premier League since it kicked off in 1992. Alan Shearer is the division's all-time leading marksman with 260 goals. But which players have the best goals per minute ratio in the top-flight?

HERE ARE THE TOP 10

10 — ALAN SHEARER

CLUBS: Blackburn Rovers, Newcastle United
GOALS: 260 Goals
MINUTES PER GOAL: 146.9 mins

Simply one of England's greatest ever strikers. Alan Shearer is the all-time Premier League leading scorer with 260 goals. The former Three Lions captain scored one every 146.9 minutes in his spells with Blackburn Rovers and Newcastle United. Shearer won the Premier League title with Rovers in 1995 and three Golden Boot Awards (1995, 1996, 1997) in his career.

9 — DIEGO COSTA

CLUBS: Chelsea
GOALS: 52 Goals
MINUTES PER GOAL: 145.19 mins

Diego Costa only played in England for three years but he certainly made a big impact. The Spain international scored 52 times in the Premier League at a rate of one every 145.19 minutes. His goals helped the Blues win two titles and his physical style of play scared many defenders. Costa left Stamford Bridge in 2017 to return to his former club Atletico Madrid.

8 — EDIN DZEKO

CLUBS: Manchester City
GOALS: 50 Goals
MINUTES PER GOAL: 141.6 mins

Edin Dzeko reached 50 Premier League goals in his five years at Manchester City. The Bosnia and Herzegovina star scored on average one every 141.6 minutes. One of those was a vital equaliser against QPR (before Aguero's winner) to help City win their first title in 2012. Dzeko won another Premier League trophy in 2014 before moving to AS Roma in 2016.

7 — ROBIN VAN PERSIE

CLUBS: Arsenal, Manchester United
GOALS: 144 Goals
MINUTES PER GOAL: 139.7 mins

Robin van Persie was known for scoring lots of spectacular goals. The Dutchman hit the back of the net 144 times in the top-flight in his time with Arsenal and Manchester United. These flew in at a rate of one every 139.7 minutes. Robin won the Golden Boot in 2012 and in 2013 – the same year he won the Premier League title with the Red Devils.

6 LUIS SUAREZ

CLUBS: Liverpool
GOALS: 69 Goals
MINUTES PER GOAL: 138.8 mins

Luis Suarez was not only a top goalscorer but an all-round world-class player. The Uruguayan master scored 69 Premier League goals at a rate of one every 138.8 minutes in three-and-a-half seasons with Liverpool. Suarez won the 2013/14 Golden Boot when the Reds came so close to winning the title. After missing out on the trophy the forward moved to Barcelona where he continued scoring for fun.

5 RUUD VAN NISTELROOY

CLUBS: Manchester United
GOALS: 95 Goals
MINUTES PER GOAL: 128.8 mins

Ruud van Nistelrooy was a goal machine in his five-year spell at Manchester United. The Dutchman scored 95 top-flight goals in 150 matches at a rate of one every 128.8 minutes. A real goal poacher RvN only scored two from outside the penalty area for the Red Devils. In the 2002/03 season he won the Golden Boot as he fired United to their eighth Premier League title. He left for Real Madrid in 2006 where he regularly carried on hitting the back of the net.

4 MOHAMED SALAH

CLUBS: Chelsea, Liverpool
GOALS: 72 Goals
MINUTES PER GOAL: 124.46 mins

Mo Salah is currently one of the sharpest shooters in the Premier League. But it has taken the Egyptian King two attempts to make it in England. The forward joined Chelsea in January 2014 but scored just twice in 13 matches. After starring at Roma he moved to Liverpool in June 2017 and hasn't looked back. Salah has netted 72 goals in 113 top-flight games at an average of one every 124.46 minutes. The two-time Golden Boot winner also holds the record for the most goals in a 38-match Premier League season with 32 in 2017/18.

3 THIERRY HENRY

CLUBS: Arsenal
GOALS: 175 Goals
MINUTES PER GOAL: 121.8 mins

Thierry Henry is simply a footballing legend. The 1998 World Cup winner is the second-highest scorer in Premier League history with 175 goals for Arsenal. The Frenchman scored those at the third-best rate of one every 121.8 minutes. All but one of those strikes came in his first spell in North London where he won two league titles and a record four Golden Boots. Henry's last goal for the Gunners came in a short loan spell in 2012. That took his club-record tally to 228 in all competitions.

2 HARRY KANE

CLUBS: Tottenham Hotspur
GOALS: 136 Goals
MINUTES PER GOAL: 120.7 mins

Harry Kane is Tottenham's star player and one of the deadliest finishers around. Since breaking into the Spurs team he has not stopped scoring with 136 top-flight goals since the start of the 2014/15 season. The England skipper has scored those at a rate of one every 120.7 minutes which puts him second on this list. Harry's eye for goal has seen him win two Premier League and the 2018 World Cup Golden Boot awards.

1 SERGIO AGUERO

CLUBS: Manchester City
GOALS: 180 Goals
MINUTES PER GOAL: 106.93 mins

Sergio Aguero tops the charts having scored 180 Premier League goals at a rapid rate of one every 106.93 minutes. The Argentine ace has netted all of those for Man City since joining from Atletico Madrid in 2011. The most famous of those goals came on the final day of his first season. With just seconds left on the clock he struck an injury-time winner to win City their first Premier League title. That goal took the trophy away from rivals Manchester United at the last second and started a period of dominance. Aguero and the Citizens have since won another three league titles. The South American shooter has also scored a record 12 Premier League hat-tricks but has amazingly not won the Golden Boot… yet.

All stats correct as of June 1st, 2020.

SPOT THE STARS

Eight Premier League stars are all at this match. Can you spot their faces in the crowd?

Raul Jimenez ✓ Phil Foden ✓ Ben Chilwell ✓

Callum Hudson-Odoi ✓ Mohamed Salah ✓

Harry Kane ✓ Wilfried Zaha ✓ Bernd Leno ✓

ANSWERS ON PAGE 76

KLOPP'S KOP KINGS

Jurgen Klopp has changed Liverpool into a trophy winning machine. The German took over from Brendan Rogers in October 2015. Now, five years later, they are one of the most feared teams on the planet. The Reds have won the Champions League, a first ever Club World Cup and their first league title in 30 years. To celebrate their success, Shoot takes a look at Liverpool's recent achievements under Klopp.

RECORD:
(SINCE LOSING 2018 CHAMPIONS LEAGUE FINAL)

Matches: 99
Wins: 75
Draws: 11
Defeats: 13

TROPHIES

2019/20 Premier League
2019 Club World Cup
2019/20 European Super Cup
2018/19 Champions League

2018 / 19
LEAGUE POSITION

Position: 2nd
Points: 97
Goals scored: 89
Goals against: 22

MEMORABLE MATCHES

LIVERPOOL 1-0 NAPOLI
Champions League group stage
11/12/2018 - Anfield

Liverpool needed a win against a tough Napoli side just to progress to the last-16 at Anfield. Salah scored in the first half but goalkeeper Alisson Becker was the hero when he miraculously saved Arkadiusz Milik's shot in the 92nd minute. The Reds went through and went on to win their sixth European Cup.

LIVERPOOL 4-0 BARCELONA
(Liverpool win 4-3 on aggregate)
Champions League semi-final
second-leg
7/5/2019 - Anfield

Liverpool needed to beat the mighty Messi and Barcelona by four goals to progress to the Champions League final. Two goals either side of half-time by Divock Origi (via a brilliant Alexander-Arnold corner) and substitute Georginio Wijnaldum sent Anfield crazy and the Reds through. It was simply one of the most magical nights in Champions League history.

LIVERPOOL 3-1 MANCHESTER CITY
Premier League
10/11/2019 - Anfield

Two goals in the first 13 minutes by Fabinho and Mohamed Salah blew the defending champions away. Sadio Mane headed in a third to strike a decisive blow to their rivals in the Premier League title race. It was the victory which got Liverpool fans believing that it would be their season.

HOW WELL DO YOU KNOW 2019 / 20?

COMPLETE THE TITLE WINNING STATS...

Position: 1st

Points: 97

Goals scored: 101

Goals against: 40

GOALS:

1. Mohamed Salah — 23
2. Roberto Firmino — 14
3. Sadio Mane — 12

ASSISTS:

1. Trent Alexander-Arnold — 16
2. Andy Robertson — 12
3. Mo Salah — 9

SUPER STATS (SO FAR)

Went 44 Premier League matches undefeated before losing at Watford in February.

Have not lost a Premier League match at Anfield in 57 matches. Last home defeat was against Crystal Palace in April 2017.

Trent Alexander-Arnold broke the Premier League record for most assists from a defender in the 2018/19 season. He recorded 12 to beat Leighton Baines' high in 2010/11.

Liverpool won the Premier League with seven games to spare. This makes it the fastest ever top-flight title victory.

FINAL WINS

CHAMPIONS LEAGUE FINAL – 1/6/2019

Liverpool 2-0 Tottenham Hotspur
Wanda Metropolitano Stadium, Madrid

It only took the Reds two minutes to score the first goal when Mohamed Salah scored a penalty past Huge Lloris. The Reds sealed their sixth European cup in the 87th minute when Divock Origi fired home.

EUROPEAN SUPER CUP FINAL – 14/8/2019

Liverpool 2-2 Chelsea
(Liverpool win 5-4 on penalties)
Vodafone Park Stadium, Istanbul

Sadio Mane scored both of Liverpool's goals. The first came in the 56th minute and the second in extra-time. It was then back-up goalkeeper Adrian's turn to become the hero. The Spaniard saved from Chelsea's Tammy Abraham in the penalty shootout to secure victory for the Reds.

WORLD CLUB CUP FINAL – 21/12/2019

Flamengo 0-1 Liverpool (AET)
Khalifa International Stadium, Doha

Liverpool won this trophy for the first time when Roberto Firmino tucked away a magical low cross from Trent Alexander-Arnold in extra-time. Goals from Naby Keita and Firmino helped the Reds beat Mexican side Monterrey 2-1 in the semi-finals.

STANDOUT STARS

TRENT ALEXANDER-ARNOLD

Position: Right-back
Date of Birth: 7/10/1998
Nationality: England

The hometown boy broke into the first-team in the 2017/18 season and is now one of the best right-backs in the world. Alexander-Arnold' crossing and passing range has caused havoc to opposing teams and he is an invaluable part of Klopp's side.

MOHAMED SALAH

Position: Forward
Date of Birth: 15/6/1992
Nationality: Egypt

The Egyptian King had a lot of doubters when he first arrived at Liverpool in 2017 but he has been nothing short of brilliant. Salah's pace, dribbling and goalscoring ability has made him the fourth fastest player to reach 50 goals in the Premier League. He is a constant threat along with Sadio Mane on the other wing.

VIRGIL VAN DIJK

Position: Centre-back
Date of Birth: 8/7/1991
Nationality: Netherlands

Only Van Dijk could be signed as the most expensive defender in football history but still be a bargain. The Dutchman has pace, strength, composure and an unbelievable passing range. Is now regarded as the best centre-back in the world.

SALAH FIRMINO OR MANE?

How well do you know Liverpool's famous front-three? Read the 15 facts below and tell us whether they are about Mohamed Salah, Roberto Firmino or Sadio Mane..?

If you think the answer is **Mohamed Salah** - Put the letter **S** in the circle.

If you think the answer is **Roberto Firmino** - Put the letter **F** in the circle.

If you think the answer is **Sadio Mane** - Put the letter **M** in the circle.

1 I have also played in the Premier League for Chelsea. *S*

2 I scored the fastest Premier League hat-trick (two minutes and 56 seconds). *M*

3 I was the first of the three to join Liverpool. *F*

4 I was the only player to play in the knockout round at the 2018 World Cup. *F*

5 I started my professional career in France. *M*

6 My goal against rivals Everton won the 2018 Puskas Award. *S*

7 I am older than the other two. *S*

8 I also played with Virgil van Dijk at my old club.

M

9 I scored the winning goal in the 2019 World Club Cup final.

F

11 I scored my first Liverpool goal against Arsenal.

M

10 I have scored the most international goals.

S

12 I won the Copa America trophy with my country in 2019.

F

13 I was named the PFA Player of the Year in 2018.

S

14 My international team wears a white and green kit.

M

15 I have the nickname 'Bobby'.

F

SHOOT'S SUPER QUIZ

FIRST HALF

Do you think you know your football? Then put your knowledge to the test in the first half of our ultimate quiz. You get one point for each correct answer.

1

Which new MLS club does former England captain David Beckham own?

Miami Star

2

Which country does Liverpool star Sadio Mane play for?

Senegal

3

Name this Bayern Munich and Germany star…

Jerome Boateng

4

Manchester United signed Daniel James from which club?

Swanse City

5

Which manager left Northern Ireland to manage Stoke City in 2020?

Mc Scott

6

Where do Queens Park Rangers play their home matches?

Loftus Road

7

Which German club are known as BVB?

Borussia Dortmund

8

This player transferred from PSV to Tottenham in January 2020….

PSV Eindoven

9

Which striker has played for Real Madrid, Napoli, Juventus, AC Milan and Chelsea?

Oliver Giroud

10

Who scored Manchester City's second goal in their 2020 League Cup final win against Aston Villa?

Foden

11

Which country are the club Getafe from?

Spein

12

Name this 2018 World Cup winner...

Antaine Griesmann

13

V's ?

Which team would Norwich City play against in the East Anglian derby?

Ipswich

14

Wayne Rooney played for this American club before moving to Derby County?

DC United

15

Which football club are nicknamed the Hornets?

Watford

16

Who was the only current Leicester City player in the 2018 England World Cup squad?

Jamie Vardy

17

Which club has won a record 13 FA Cups?

Arsenal

18

Who scored Liverpool's winning goal in the 2019 Club World Cup Final?

Firminio

19

Name this stadium which has a capacity of 32,702....

The stadium of light

20

Chelsea midfielder Billy Gilmour is from which country?

Scotland

SECOND HALF KICKS OFF ON PAGE 68.

ANSWERS ON PAGE 76

33

FAMOUS FANS

You will find that almost every football club has a celebrity fan. Here we reveal who stars from the worlds of royalty, music, film, TV, and sport root for.

PRINCE WILLIAM
(ROYALTY)
ASTON VILLA

AMANDA HOLDEN
(TV)
EVERTON

LEWIS HAMILTON
(F1)
ARSENAL

DANIEL CRAIG
(ACTOR)
LIVERPOOL

ADELE
(MUSIC)
TOTTENHAM HOTSPUR

JIMMY ANDERSON
(CRICKET)
BURNLEY

STORMZY
(MUSIC)
MANCHESTER
UNITED

ANT AND DEC
(TV)
NEWCASTLE
UNITED

MARGOT ROBBIE
(ACTOR)
FULHAM

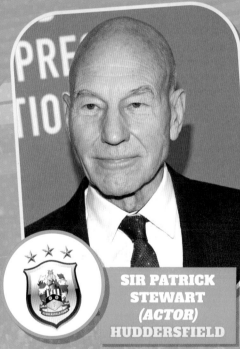

SIR ELTON JOHN
(MUSIC)
WATFORD

KEIRA KNIGHTLEY
(ACTOR)
WEST HAM UNITED

**SIR PATRICK
STEWART**
(ACTOR)
HUDDERSFIELD

NATALIE DORMER
(ACTOR)
CHELSEA

JAMES MCAVOY
(ACTOR)
CELTIC

RAFAEL NADAL
(TENNIS)
REAL MADRID

SUPER
>>>>>>>>>>>>

STOPPERS

The role of a goalkeeper has changed in recent years. Stoppers now need to be good with their feet and not just a safe pair of hands. There's a lot of top 'keepers around but here's Shoot's current super-six.

EDERSON MORAES

BIRTH DATE: August 17, 1993
BIRTH PLACE: Osasco, Brazil
DID YOU KNOW?: Ederson was inspired by Sao Paulo goalkeeping legend Rogerio Ceni.

The imposing Brazilian's passing is one of the best around. He often uses his left-foot to accurately spray long range balls to his teammates. Ederson was signed by Manchester City from Benfica for £35 million in 2017 and has helped the Citizens win two Premier League titles. Money well spent.

ALISSON BECKER

BIRTH DATE: October 2, 1992
BIRTH PLACE: Novo Hamburgo, Brazil
DID YOU KNOW?: Alisson likes to sing and play the guitar in his spare time.

Brazil's number 1 goalkeeper has risen to the top in recent years. His cat-like reflexes and calmness between the posts saw Liverpool pay AS Roma over £65 million to sign him in 2018. Eyebrows were raised but Champions League, Club World Cup and Premier League trophies since prove that was a smart investment.

MARC-ANDRE TER STEGEN

BIRTH DATE: April 30, 1992
BIRTH PLACE: Monchengladbach, Germany
DID YOU KNOW?: Ter Stegen started out playing as a striker before taking over from an injured goalkeeper when he was 10.

Barcelona's brick wall seems to be getting better with age. Ter Stegen has fantastic shot-stopping skills but can also play with the ball at his feet. He has won every trophy there is to win since moving to the Camp Nou from hometown club Borussia Monchengladbach in 2014. There's a real battle going on between the Barca star and Manuel Neuer for Germany's number 1 shirt.

JAN OBLAK

BIRTH DATE: January 7, 1993
BIRTH PLACE: Skofja Loka, Slovenia
DID YOU KNOW?: Oblak's older sister, Teja, plays professional basketball for Slovenia.

The towering Slovenian is a real presence between the sticks. Atletico Madrid's star stopper is great at coming off his line, commanding the box and saving shots. Oblak has played a key part in his club's success under Diego Simeone and was named La Liga's best goalkeeper four seasons in a row.

THIBAUT COURTOIS

BIRTH DATE: May 11, 1992
BIRTH PLACE: Bree, Belgium
DID YOU KNOW?: Courtois was awarded the Golden Glove award for best goalkeeper at the 2018 World Cup.

The Real Madrid stopper has been playing at the elite level for nearly a decade. Courtois is very good one-on-one and has excellent agility. He first showed this at Atletico Madrid where he won four trophies and reached a Champions League final. The Belgian then starred in two Premier League title victories with Chelsea before moving to Spain in 2018.

GIANLUIGI DONNARUMMA

BIRTH DATE: February 25, 1999
BIRTH PLACE: Castellammare di Stabia, Italy
DID YOU KNOW?: Donnarumma's older brother, Antonio, is also a goalkeeper for AC Milan.

Five years after becoming the youngest goalkeeper to start a Serie A match the 'keeper has now played over 200 matches for his boyhood club AC Milan. His mental strength, composure and technique also saw him become the youngest stopper to play for Italy. There's no doubting Donnarumma is the long-term replacement to legend Gianluigi Buffon.

NEW KIDS ON THE ≫≫≫≫≫ BLOCK

Every season a new crop of talented young stars make the breakthrough and challenge the best players around. Here's eight who have the potential to play at the top level for many, many years.

CURTIS JONES

POSITION: Midfielder
DATE OF BIRTH: January 30, 2001

FACT

Became Liverpool's youngest captain at 19 years and 5 days in February 2020.

GABRIEL MARTINELLI

POSITION: Striker
DATE OF BIRTH: June 18, 2001

FACT

Liverpool boss Jurgen Klopp has described him as the ''talent of the century''.

MICHAEL OBAFEMI

POSITION: Striker
DATE OF BIRTH: July 6, 2000

FACT

Is Southampton's youngest ever Premier League goalscorer.

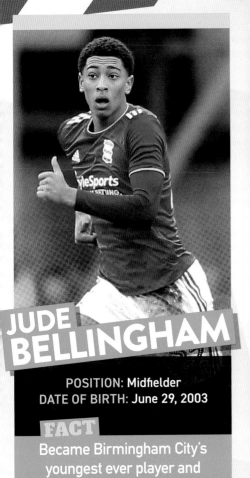

JUDE BELLINGHAM

POSITION: Midfielder
DATE OF BIRTH: June 29, 2003

FACT

Became Birmingham City's youngest ever player and goalscorer in the 2019/20 season.

JEREMY NGAKIA

POSITION: Full-back
DATE OF BIRTH: September 7, 2000

FACT

Had a trial with Chelsea before joining West Ham United when he was 14 years old.

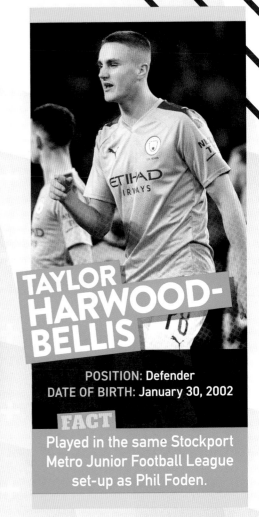

TAYLOR HARWOOD-BELLIS

POSITION: Defender
DATE OF BIRTH: January 30, 2002

FACT

Played in the same Stockport Metro Junior Football League set-up as Phil Foden.

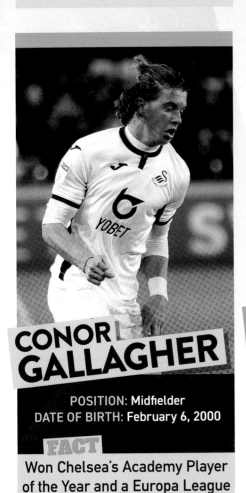

CONOR GALLAGHER

POSITION: Midfielder
DATE OF BIRTH: February 6, 2000

FACT

Won Chelsea's Academy Player of the Year and a Europa League winners' medal in 2019.

NATHAN FERGUSON

POSITION: Full-back
DATE OF BIRTH: October 6, 2000

FACT

Moved from Jamaica to Aston (Birmingham) before signing for West Brom when he was eight years old.

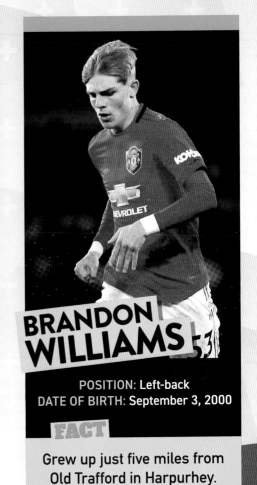

BRANDON WILLIAMS

POSITION: Left-back
DATE OF BIRTH: September 3, 2000

FACT

Grew up just five miles from Old Trafford in Harpurhey.

England have become one of the best international women's teams on the planet in recent years.

The Lionesses reached the semi-finals of both the 2015 and 2019 World Cups, plus the 2017 European Championship.

One of the standout players and headline makers of those tournaments and over the past five years is Lucy Bronze.

After winning numerous titles in England, the attacking full-back moved to European champions Lyon in 2017.

Since flying out to France she has won two Champions Leagues, two French league titles and became the first English player to win the UEFA Women's Player of the Year Award.

Lucy spoke to Shoot about playing for Europe's best club team, those incredible World Cup journeys, being named Europe's best player, and how studying in America inspired her to continue with football.

Q: What are your earliest footballing memories?

"My brother was obsessed with football, and I was obsessed with being like him. We all used to play football in the garden, in the streets at night and then at school. I don't think I met another girl who played until I was about 11 years old. I never really thought anything of it because we were just kids and we all loved playing football with each other."

Q: Who were your sporting idols?

"Kelly Smith is the one who inspired me when I was breaking through. I watched her and I loved the way she played football. She was one of the best in the world at the time and a far better player than I will ever be. I also admired women in other sports. Dame Kelly Holmes and Paula Radcliffe were two I looked up to. They worked so hard and were very successful."

FACT FILE

POSITION: **RIGHT-BACK**
HEIGHT: **1.72M (5FT 8IN)**
BIRTH DATE: **OCTOBER 28, 1991**
BIRTH PLACE: **BERWICK UPON-TWEED**

LUCY BRONZE

Q: How did you become a defender?

"When I played for a boys' team they always wanted to be the attackers but I was just happy to play. So the easiest option for the manager was to put me as a full-back. When I played for my first girls' team I was actually a striker. The size I am now was the size I was at 13 years old. Lucy Staniforth (Birmingham City and England) used to play for the same team in midfield and whip crosses into me."

Q: What was it like to go to America to study in 2009?

"That was the best thing I've ever done. The women's league has really taken off in England, but America was the place to be. When I was in England, I was bag packing in supermarkets just so I could pay for my bus ticket to get to games. I had everything in North Carolina. I was studying alongside playing and training every single day, plus I also played with players who have now gone on and won World Cups. It really helped me decide what I wanted to do."

Q: You moved to Lyon in 2017. Was it a tough decision to move away from England?

"There were some things I did not want to leave behind but it was actually an easy decision. I was settled at Man City but the only team I would have gone abroad for was Lyon. I wasn't sure I would be good enough for them but when the opportunity came along it was a no brainer. They are the best team in Europe, have won lots of trophies and have all the best players. I wanted to win the Champions League and keep improving. I have done that so it was the right decision and I haven't looked back."

Q: What are the training sessions like at Lyon with so many top players?

"I never get nervous before matches but I was before my first week training with Lyon. I wanted to prove myself to all the world-class players here. Some of the sessions are tougher than matches I play. At training we play 11 vs 11 and both sets of midfields could easily play in any other team in the world."

Q: How does living in France compare with England?

"It's definitely a more relaxed lifestyle in France and the weather is great. I'm normally sitting outside in the sun on my couch most days. At Lyon we have fresh baguettes every single day and I must go through hundreds of them. I have enjoyed getting to know their culture and trying so many new things."

Q: What do you think of the FA Women's Super League in England?

"The League is probably one of the best in terms of how good the teams are as a collective. They have some of the most competitive games and the top-three teams always compete well in the Champions League. I've played two English teams since I've been at Lyon and they have been the toughest games I have played. I think the WSL will probably be the best league in a few years' time, especially after the Euros (2022) in England."

Q: What was it like to reach the 2015 and 2019 World Cup semi-finals with England?

"Canada 2015 was my first ever World Cup so it was definitely my most exciting. We were so far away from home and we have never really been successful in World Cups so everything came together. Last year was special for me personally as I was playing in France and had the chance to play at Lyon's home ground in the semi-final. I was disappointed that we were not able to get to the final but England used to struggle to get out of the groups. Now we are a side that has got to the semi-finals twice. It was gutting but shows we know what we are doing. We just need to take that next step now."

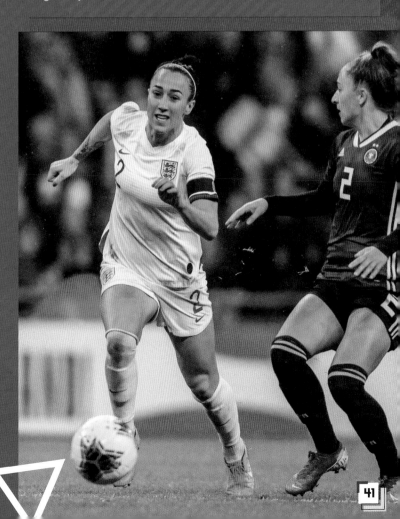

Q: What do you think the future looks like for England?

"Younger players are taking the shirts of the older players now and we have a really good mix of talent in the squad. There is a new generation of English players coming through. Many of these players probably would have been inspired by our run to the semi-finals in 2015. I think there will be more young girls watching future England sides on the TV who go on to play with their heroes."

Q: What was it like to become the first English player to win the UEFA Player of the Year award?

"It was a huge surprise and I was grateful to have been nominated. I was up against two of my Lyon teammates, Ada Hegerberg and Amandine Henry, which was really funny and interesting. I think it is good we have English players getting recognised in that way, and it will inspire loads of younger players."

Q: How much are you looking forward to possibly taking part in the 2021 Olympics?

"I didn't get the chance to play in the 2012 Olympics and then we were not allowed to play at the Rio Olympics. So having missed out on the last two I really want to go. I think we could be the team to beat as we have so many great players in Great Britain. It will be very hard to get into the squad with all of the talent we have but hopefully I can stay fit and get picked. I would want a gold medal. I cannot be getting a bronze again."

Q: You've played in midfield for England at times. Could that become a permanent position for you?

"I used to play midfield and I enjoyed it but I think it is quite difficult to move positions now as I am in my late 20s. I had a lot of fun playing midfield for England and I feel we had some good performances. I also played with younger players like Georgia Stanway and Keira Walsh so I became more of a leader. I hope I was able to help them in some way."

Q: Do you have a career highlight?

"Playing in my first World Cup. Our first knockout game was against Norway and we went 1-0 down and then I scored a goal from outside the box. I had never scored a goal from outside of the box in my life at the time. I feel my life changed from that moment. My confidence grew as well because I did not expect to ever score the winning goal in a World Cup knockout game for England. It was a real turning point for me in my career."

Q: Do you have any advice for any young readers who dream of becoming footballers?

"Even though I have won lots of awards, I don't think I'm naturally the most talented footballer. Everything people see in me is all hard work. I know everyone always says 'work hard' but it's true and that's what I do every single day. I would also say enjoy yourself. If you are happy doing something then you are more likely to work hard at it. That is how I have lived and worked all throughout my career."

IN FOCUS

One thing you miss about not living in England:
Speaking English all of the time.

Toughest player you've faced:
Kelly Smith. My head hurt after.

Favourite TV boxset:
Brooklyn Nine-Nine. It's so funny!

Most played artist on your playlist:
Probably Drake.

Favourite football shirt:
The Red Lionesses shirt we still wear now.

KIT SWAP

These four players have had their kit mixed up. They really need your help.
Can you return the shirts, shorts and socks to their owner?

A

B

C

D

A

B

C

D

A

B
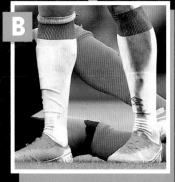

C

D
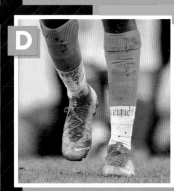

ODSONNE EDOUARD	KEVIN DE BRUYNE	RUBEN NEVES	RICHARLISON
SHIRT C	SHIRT D	SHIRT B	SHIRT A
SHORTS D	SHORTS A	SHORTS D	SHORTS C
SOCKS D	SOCKS C	SOCKS A	SOCKS B

ANSWERS ON PAGE 76

Q: How strong would the Team GB squad be next summer?

"With only 18 players to pick, the competition for a place will be tough. For instance, the 23 that went to the World Cup with England will have to be cut by five and then there is still Scotland, Northern Ireland and Wales thrown into that. It's a bit of a headache for the manager."

Q: Before the World Cup you signed for Man City. How are you enjoying it there?

"I am really loving it. The girls are great, as are the staff and the facilities. It's been a great transition for me as well moving to a new house, new city and getting to grips with Manchester. It's been great and getting to work and train with so many great players has been really good so far."

Q: What is it like to train and play at the amazing Etihad Campus?

"The pitches are beautiful and second to none. Even in snow and ice we are still able to go out and train. The gym is unbelievable, and we are able to do stuff in there to help us on the pitch and with recovery. I am very lucky to have an ice bath straight after training which means I don't have to come home and buy hundreds of bags of ice like I used to. We also get nutrition, breakfast and lunch, so we are really privileged and in such an amazing place. It's a place where we can try to be on the top of our game, improve ourselves and hopefully win something as well."

Q: You hadn't won a trophy since 2013. Was that a big reason in moving to Man City from Birmingham?

"I had a great time at Birmingham and won WSL top goalscorer with them. But I wanted to potentially put myself in a position to win trophies and to be fighting at the top of the league. The chance to play in the Champions League really drew me as well. Although it didn't go as well as we hoped for the first time the whole exposure and travelling to play is such an incredible experience."

Q: You are one of the top strikers in WSL history but what makes a good goalscorer?

"Phil Neville (England manager) always tells me that being within the width of the goal is the main thing. I think it all starts on the training field really. Not just doing shooting drills where someone sets you up and you shoot, but working on the awkward finishes. Make it so the balls aren't quite right, so you're having to move your body and use different parts to score. Work on finishing with your head, left foot, right foot, one touch and more. It's about going a bit outside the box on how you're developing your finishing and your movement. That is really key."

Q: You are only 10 behind Kelly Smith's England goal record. That must be a target of yours?

"I've only really known that recently. Somebody did ask me how many goals I've scored and I didn't have a scooby. What Kelly achieved for England, the amount of goals she scored, the number of caps she had, what she did for our team and our country was incredible. To even be near that number is great. I just absolutely love playing for England. I'm super patriotic so any chance that I get to contribute or score is amazing for me."

Q: What do you like to do when you're not playing football?

"I love going for coffee. Sitting, chatting, not talking about football, speaking about family life or anything else. I think it's nice just to really have a bit of time away from football. I like watching boxsets and going for walks in the Derbyshire area."

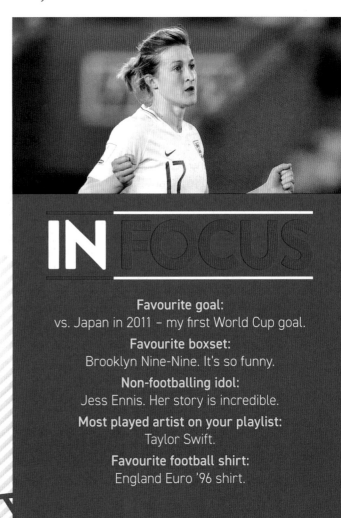

IN FOCUS

Favourite goal:
vs. Japan in 2011 – my first World Cup goal.

Favourite boxset:
Brooklyn Nine-Nine. It's so funny.

Non-footballing idol:
Jess Ennis. Her story is incredible.

Most played artist on your playlist:
Taylor Swift.

Favourite football shirt:
England Euro '96 shirt.

READY TO ROAR

After reaching the last two World Cup semi-finals it's fair to say England have one of the best women's teams in the world. Led by captain Steph Houghton, the Lionesses' squad is full of experience and quality. But with one eye on Euro 2022 (in England!) here's some promising stars who have what it takes to become leading Lionesses.

ELLIE ROEBUCK

Roebuck has quickly established herself as one of the best young goalkeepers around. By the age of just 21, she had already helped Manchester City win five domestic trophies. The Sheffield-born stopper represented England at Under-17, 19 and 20 levels before making her senior debut in 2018.

BIRTH DATE: SEPT 23, 1999
ENGLAND DEBUT: Vs AUSTRIA, NOVEMBER 8TH, 2018

LEAH WILLIAMSON

Williamson has been with Arsenal since the age of nine and made her debut for the club in 2014. She started her career as a midfielder before moving to defence where she has helped the Gunners win five trophies. The ball-playing defender has represented England from Under-15s level and is a potential future captain.

BIRTH DATE: MARCH 29, 1997
ENGLAND DEBUT: Vs RUSSIA, JUNE 8TH, 2018

GEORGIA STANWAY

BIRTH DATE: JAN 1, 1999
ENGLAND DEBUT: Vs AUSTRIA, NOVEMBER 8TH, 2018

Stanway has caught the eye since joining Manchester City from Blackburn Rovers in 2015. A tricky forward who has a real eye for goal, she has already won five trophies with the Blues. The playmaker scored on her Lionesses debut and made five appearances at the 2019 World Cup.

CHLOE KELLY

Kelly started her career at Arsenal before moving to Everton on loan in 2016. The forward has stayed with the Toffees and is now their star player. In the 2019/20 season she scored nine goals before the season was ended. That form earned her an England recall who she has played for since Under-15s level.

BIRTH DATE: JAN 15, 1998
ENGLAND DEBUT: Vs AUSTRIA, NOVEMBER 8TH, 2018

LAUREN HEMP

Hemp has enjoyed a rapid rise over the past couple of years since moving to Manchester City in 2018. Just over a year later and the fearless forward had made her senior international debut and won two domestic trophies with the Citizens. The Norfolk-born attacker was also named England Young Player of the Year in 2017.

BIRTH DATE: AUG 7, 2000
ENGLAND DEBUT: Vs PORTUGAL, OCTOBER 8TH, 2019

FACT FILE

POSITION: **MIDFIELDER**
HEIGHT: **1.78M (5FT 10IN)**
BIRTH DATE: **JANUARY 10, 1999**
BIRTH PLACE: **PORTSMOUTH**

MASON
MOUNT

Chelsea are enjoying a fresh start under the management of their very own club legend, Frank Lampard.

The Blues have handed first-team opportunities to a number of young, exciting players and are playing attractive football.

One of those talented stars is Mason Mount, who joined the London club at the age of six.

After starring on loan at Derby County (where the midfielder played under Lampard), he became a Chelsea regular and England international in the 2019/20 season.

Shoot spoke to Mason about his Stamford Bridge breakthrough, his childhood football memories and representing his country.

Q: What are your earliest footballing memories?

"I've always been around football. My dad was a manager at Newport (Isle of Wight) so I remember going to the games from two years old. On the pitch, after games, in the dressing room, I was everywhere. I also remember going to Pompey for the first time when I was about five or six. I used to play for my local team in Portsmouth before signing for Chelsea."

Q: So would you say your dad played a big part in your development?

"Definitely! Him being a football man pushed me to want to be involved. Growing up I didn't really know anything else. I remember kicking balls around the house 24/7 and my mum telling me off for smashing things. I've still got the videos of me kicking the ball around everywhere."

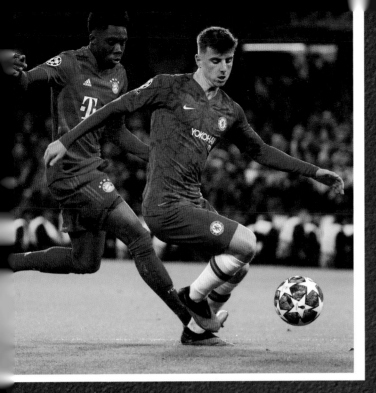

do it together is special and doesn't happen often. I'm close to Tammy and all the academy boys and we have to pinch ourselves now and again. The Champions League games are crazy because we used to ball-boy those matches. Now we're playing in those games, that's quite surreal."

Q: What is it like to now be a Premier League regular?

"It's an absolute dream. Getting an opportunity to progress on the top stage at a club I love is brilliant. I've wanted to show all the coaches that have helped me what I can do because I wouldn't be where I am without everyone I've worked under. This season has not just been a proud moment for me but for my family and everyone else involved."

Q: You're a midfielder who likes to get forward and score goals. What skills do you need to play that role?

"You have to make that run past the opposition midfielder to get into the box and want to score. The amount of times you can get into the box and get in good positions increases your chance of scoring or assisting. I'd also say work on your finishing as you can never be too good at scoring goals. Don't forget that defending for the team is also important. The games are played at such a high tempo you've got to be switched on and have good fitness levels."

Q: How proud are you to have represented and scored for England at senior level?

"I still don't really believe it. Even when people say it, I think 'did I score?' It's an absolute blur that I scored, I can't even remember what happened. I started at Under-16s with England and there's loads of players. You really work through the ages so I'm very proud and honoured to represent my country. Every time I put the shirt on I want to do better than last time. To play and to score made my family so proud. It's a dream come true."

Q: Who were your idols growing up?

"My dad was a massive Manchester United fan so I always used to love David Beckham. I used to be a winger actually so I was always on the free kicks trying to whip the ball in like him. At Chelsea, Frank Lampard, John Terry, Didier Drogba and Joe Cole were a massive inspiration. Just watching them all play when I was growing up there was brilliant."

Q: How much did loans at Vitesse and Derby County help you?

"I think they were massive learning curves and turning points for my career. I went to Vitesse a boy and became a man. I went from Under-23s football to first-team but also had to look after myself off the pitch in another country. The Championship with Derby was also tough but I got to show people in England that I could play here. If I didn't have those loans I wouldn't be the player I am now."

Q: You played for Frank Lampard at Derby and now at Chelsea. What's he like as a manager?

"It's been brilliant to work with him. When he phoned me there was no other option in my head than joining Derby on loan to try and learn as much as I can. The opportunity to work with an idol and a club legend doesn't come around often so I took it with both hands. Since he's come back to Chelsea it's been brilliant. He gives everything for the club and his passion rubs off on the whole squad. He works with us on the field with other coaches like Jody and Joe Edwards which has helped us younger players settle. I'm playing a lot of matches and learning from him every day."

Q: How great is it to be playing in the first-team with other academy graduates like Tammy Abraham, Fikayo Tomori, Reece James and Callum Hudson-Odoi?

"Getting into the first-team and playing games has always been the end goal for all of us. So to come through and

Q: Gareth Southgate has been great since taking the job. What's he been like with you?

"He's been brilliant with me. I think my first meeting with him was when I was in the youth teams and he was very involved with all the younger groups coming through. I was maybe playing for the Under-17s when I first spoke to him and he was asking questions about how I was doing. He actually wants to know what you're like as a person, not just on the pitch. He then invited me to the training camp before the 2018 World Cup. To see how they prepared for the tournament was an unbelievable experience and that set me up for the next couple of years. For him to then put the faith in me by playing me has meant so much to me."

Q: What's it been like to be in the England squad with your good friend Declan Rice?

"We've been friends for about 14 years, ever since we were at Chelsea. We have always stayed close and talk basically every day – he's one of my best mates. To grow up together but then both play in the Premier League is incredible. But then for both of us to be playing on the same Wembley pitch for England was a dream."

Q: How exciting is the prospect of playing for England at Euro 2021?

"It's a massive goal of mine. It would mean so much to every single player to win a major tournament with England. I was able to do that at Under-19 level which has given me a taste of what it can be like. There's so much competition in the squad and that's brilliant as it keeps upping the level. If we carry on this path and keep developing as a young, hungry team, we can definitely achieve it."

Q: What advice would you give to any reader who dreams of becoming a footballer?

"You've got to set goals and targets for yourself. If you put your mind to the goal and really focus on achieving them than you can. From a young age, I knew I wanted to play for Chelsea and I wanted to play for England. I didn't let anyone take my focus off that or put me down. If you stay driven and work hard on your game, you can achieve anything."

Q: Did you have any setbacks growing up?

"In my first session with Chelsea Under-16s I cracked my femur. I was out for a couple of months and I missed maybe half of the season. It was tough but it really helped me to become stronger mentally and work on other aspects of my game. So any setback you get you need to stay positive and look at what you can work on."

Q: What do you like to do when you're not training or playing?

"I'm a massive gamer, so I love to play. I've always been into that from a young age and my go-to game is Call of Duty. Me and Dec (Declan Rice) have been playing that loads recently. We have a bit of a squad going on with Ryan Fredericks also playing as well."

IN FOCUS

Favourite away stadium you've played in:
Stadio Olimpico (Rome)

Favourite boxset:
Money Heist and Peaky Blinders.

Best gamer at Chelsea:
Christian Pulisic. Tammy will be gutted.

Most played artist on your playlist:
Drake, DaBaby and Travis Scott

Favourite football shirt:
Chelsea's retro FA Cup shirt (2019/20)

BLUE IS THE FUTURE

Frank Lampard has shown real belief in younger players since taking charge at Chelsea. Here's a closer look at Mason's mates who have also made the step from academy to first-team.

TAMMY ABRAHAM

POSITION: STRIKER

DATE OF BIRTH: OCTOBER 2, 1997

NATIONALITY: ENGLISH

JOINED CHELSEA: 2004

CHELSEA DEBUT: MAY 2016 VS LIVERPOOL

FACT: CHELSEA'S TOP SCORER IN THE 2019/20 SEASON.

FIKAYO TOMORI

POSITION: DEFENDER

DATE OF BIRTH: DECEMBER 19, 1997

NATIONALITY: ENGLISH

JOINED CHELSEA: 2005

CHELSEA DEBUT: MAY 2016 VS LEICESTER CITY

FACT: UNDER-20 WORLD CUP WINNER WITH ENGLAND IN 2017.

CALLUM HUDSON-ODOI

POSITION: WINGER

DATE OF BIRTH: NOVEMBER 7, 2000

NATIONALITY: ENGLISH

JOINED CHELSEA: 2007

CHELSEA DEBUT: JANUARY 2018 VS NEWCASTLE UNITED

FACT: BAYERN MUNICH TRIED TO BUY HUDSON-ODOI IN 2019.

REECE JAMES

POSITION: RIGHT-BACK

DATE OF BIRTH: DECEMBER 8, 1999

NATIONALITY: ENGLISH

JOINED CHELSEA: 2006

CHELSEA DEBUT: SEPTEMBER 2019 VS GRIMSBY TOWN

FACT: CHELSEA'S YOUNGEST EVER CHAMPIONS LEAGUE GOALSCORER.

BILLY GILMOUR

POSITION: MIDFIELDER

DATE OF BIRTH: JUNE 11, 2001

NATIONALITY: SCOTTISH

JOINED CHELSEA: 2017

CHELSEA DEBUT: AUGUST 2019 VS SHEFFIELD UNITED

FACT: WAS IN RANGERS' ACADEMY FOR EIGHT YEARS BEFORE JOINING CHELSEA.

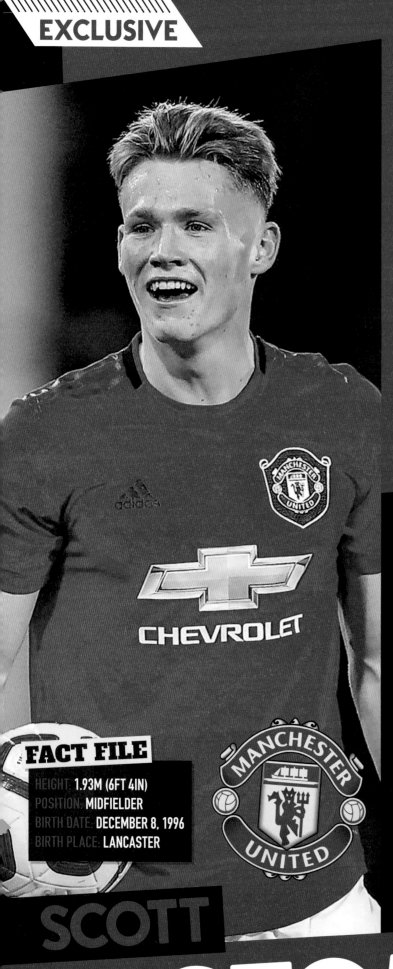

Manchester United look to be on the right track as they aim to become Premier League title contenders once again.

Ole Gunnar Solskjaer has built an exciting squad at Old Trafford where competition for a place in the starting XI is high.

Powerful midfielder Scott McTominay is one of the players the Norwegian club legend has to choose from.

The Scotland international joined the Red Devils at the age of five and has been a first-team regular since making his senior debut at the end of the 2016/17 season.

Shoot spoke to Scott about what it's like to play in this exciting United team, representing Scotland and advice on what it takes to become a professional footballer.

Did you have any players you idolised growing up?

"Paul Scholes and Zinedine Zidane. A proper mix of footballers who were absolutely incredible players and a joy to watch. I still watch them now on YouTube to help educate and improve me as a midfielder."

What was it like as a young player to come through the academy at a club the size of Manchester United?

"Coming through at a club like Manchester United was a pleasure and so enjoyable. The coaches always told me to play with a smile on my face and work as hard as I possibly can. The list of coaches who have had an amazing impact on my young career is incredible and it's a credit to the football club."

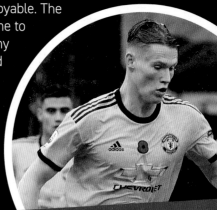

FACT FILE

HEIGHT: **1.93M (6FT 4IN)**
POSITION: **MIDFIELDER**
BIRTH DATE: **DECEMBER 8, 1996**
BIRTH PLACE: **LANCASTER**

SCOTT MCTOMINAY

Do you feel the club is on the right track to compete for the Premier League title very soon?

"That's a difficult question and one that's hard to say. All we can do as a squad is to continue to do all of the right things to get in a position to do that. Our goal is ultimately to win trophies, including the Premier League."

How proud are you to represent Scotland?

"I'm extremely proud to represent Scotland. I always look forward to the international games and pulling on the shirt. It's something that all my family are also very proud and happy about. The talent we have at various other clubs is really good at the moment. We have a foundation to build on. With the right mentality, I would definitely say we are on the correct path. But it will take dedication and for everyone to come together."

What advice would you give to any reader wanting to be a professional footballer?'

"I think that's simple. Work relentlessly, be humble and always enjoy your pathway whichever way it takes you. Do that and you won't go far wrong."

You made your debut in May 2017 and have been a first-team regular since. How does it feel to have broken through at one of the biggest clubs in the world?

"The feeling of breaking through as a young player at any football club is special, but at Manchester United it's extra special. The fans have huge expectations and it's different to playing at other football clubs. Some players don't like that but I'm somebody who is ridiculously competitive and love the challenge to perform every week. In any sport, if there's not an element of competitive edge in what I'm doing then I won't be playing to my maximum. Every game is massive at Manchester United and I love it!"

Jose Mourinho gave you your break. What was it like to be trusted by such a world-class manager?

"Jose Mourinho has had a huge influence on my career by giving me my debut. I am forever grateful for the trust and belief he had in me when we were in a difficult moment. It goes without saying I give my absolute best every single session and do anything to help the team for any manager I play for."

Ole Gunnar Solskjaer has the team playing great football. How exciting is it to play for this team?

"We are playing some terrific football and we can sense that feeling of us pushing firmly in the right direction. The coaches and the manager demand the very top standard in training every single day. The players we have all have a proper Man United personality, humble attitude and are prepared to work to be the best we can be."

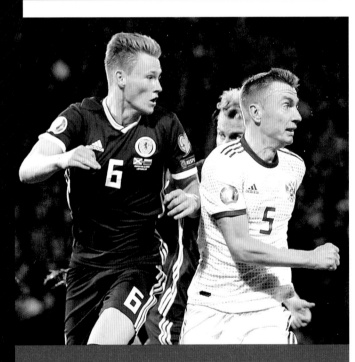

IN FOCUS

Day off activity? Golf and snooker
Most played artist on your playlist? Roddy Ricch
Favourite TV series? Drake & Josh
Best gamer at Man United? Me
Favourite football shirt?
Orange kit for my old team Halton Hotshots

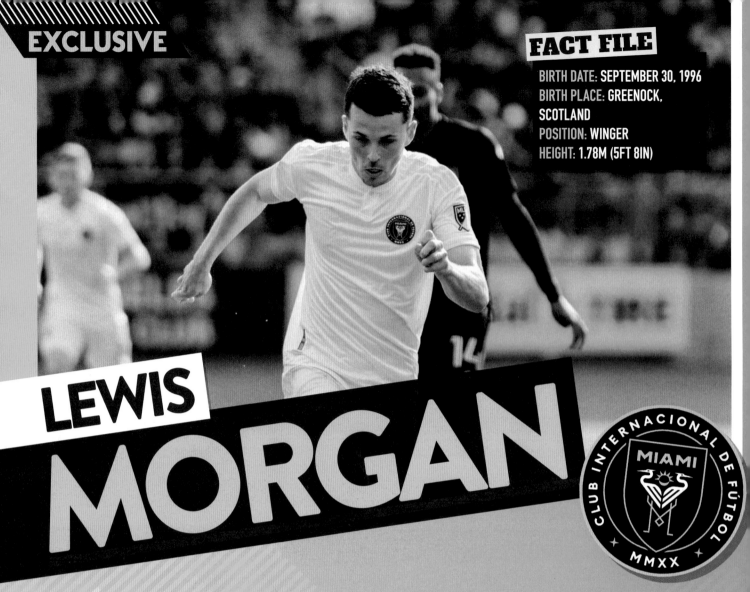

LEWIS MORGAN

In case you haven't heard, David Beckham is now the co-owner of new MLS club Inter Miami.

The former England captain's American team played their first match in March 2020 in what is sure to be a rollercoaster journey.

One player who is firmly on board and ready for the ride is Scottish winger Lewis Morgan.

The playmaker has won promotion with St Mirren and played for Celtic in Old Firm and European matches.

But after spending the end of the 2018/19 season on loan at Sunderland he snapped up the opportunity to move over 4,000 miles west to Florida.

Morgan spoke to Shoot about life so far at Inter Miami, representing his country and what it's like to be the first number 7 at Beckham's club.

Did you always know you wanted to be a footballer?

"I always got asked in school what I wanted to be and I would always say a footballer. People would always say to pick other things to do because that wouldn't happen. But for me it was always going to be football. That is probably why I am where I am today."

Which players have you always looked up to?

"Thierry Henry when he was at Arsenal in that Invincibles team. He was one of the reasons why I loved football so much as a youngster. Now I have to say Lionel Messi as he is on a completely different planet."

What was it like to represent Scotland back in 2018?

"My international debut was the proudest moment of my career so far. I played in matches against Peru and Mexico which were great experiences. There's a lot of competition for a place in the squad with a lot of good players. But if I play well regularly I back myself to break back in and hopefully add to my two caps."

Can you describe how it felt to play for Celtic?

"I didn't play as much as I would've wanted to but I don't regret it. Being lucky enough to be involved in big Old Firm and European matches at Celtic Park was really special. I have fond memories having played for such a massive club with a massive fan base and in such a fantastic stadium. It was amazing to play for Celtic."

Was it a difficult decision to move to Inter Miami in the summer of 2020?

"It was massive for me. I could've signed for clubs in England but I was at the stage where I just wanted something fresh. With the whole project here and with Beckham involved, it was something I'd regret if I didn't make the move. The league is getting a lot more competitive with the standard rising every year. Since I've been here I've been blown away by Inter Miami's ambition and what it wants to achieve. Miami is obviously also a great place to live as well."

How have you settled to life in Miami?

"I've loved the football side of things and feel like I've adapted well. It's a great place to live when it comes to the culture and lifestyle. I've also got used to the heat as it's a lot warmer out here than it is in the UK. The heat makes it a bit more challenging but I've loved every second of it so far."

Did you follow the MLS before you joined?

"I love football so I'm always checking scores from all over the world and that includes the MLS. In the last few years there's been more Scottish players coming out here so I've kept an even closer eye on it. It's getting a lot more coverage back in the UK and I think it will continue to grow. It's an exciting time and it's great to be a part of it."

David Beckham is the co-owner. What's it like being a player at his club?

"He's a great guy. The club is his vision and it means so much to him so he is very hands on. He comes to the games, the training ground and we've all had a meal with him. It's great for us to have someone who we looked up to as a player involved with the club. Coming from the UK it's even more exciting and was a massive reason why I wanted to move here."

You were also given his famous number 7 shirt. How proud are you to wear that?

"When they first told me I was going to get the number 7 shirt it was great. To be the first number 7 at his (Beckham's) Inter Miami is a massive honour for me. I know what a big part that played in his England and club career. Hopefully I can create my own legacy with the shirt now."

IN FOCUS

Favourite American sports team outside MLS?
Miami Heat

Better to drive on the left or right?
Left (but getting used to the right)

Best American music artist? Drake

Best US TV Series? US Office

One thing you are not missing about Scotland?
The rain

BIG MON£Y

TOP 10 BIGGEST TRANSFERS

7 CRISTIANO RONALDO

FROM: REAL MADRID
TO: JUVENTUS
WHEN: 2018

FEE £105.3 MILLION

The five-time Ballon d'Or winner has continued his fine form in Italy. He scored 28 goals in his first season to help Juventus win the Italian Super Cup and their eighth Serie A title in a row.

10 EDEN HAZARD

FROM: CHELSEA
TO: REAL MADRID
WHEN: 2019

FEE £90 MILLION

Hazard's much anticipated 'dream' move to Los Blancos hasn't gone to plan so far. Injuries have limited his playing time but it's too early to write off the brilliant Belgian.

6 ANTOINE GRIEZMANN

FROM: ATLETICO MADRID
TO: BARCELONA
WHEN: 2019

FEE £108 MILLION

World Cup 2018 winner Griezmann averaged a goal every other game at Atletico Madrid. Despite having to play second fiddle to Lionel Messi he has so far registered 15 goals in his debut season.

9 GARETH BALE

FROM: TOTTENHAM HOTSPUR
TO: REAL MADRID
WHEN: 2013

FEE £90 MILLION

Bale's time in Spain has been frustrating. He's actually won four Champions League trophies but has been held back by injuries and rumoured unrest with management.

5 OUSMANE DEMBELE

FROM: BORUSSIA DORTMUND
TO: BARCELONA
WHEN: 2017

FEE £112.5 MILLION

The Frenchman's big money move has been hampered by injury. Saying that he has still played a part in two La Liga title victories for the Catalan club.

8 PAUL POGBA

FROM: JUVENTUS
TO: MANCHESTER UNITED
WHEN: 2016

FEE £94.5 MILLION

The Frenchman has helped United win the League Cup and Europa League since returning to Old Trafford in 2016. Despite having his critics, United are a better side with him in the midfield.

TRANSFER TIMELINE

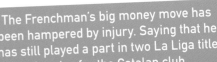

FIRST EVER TRANSFER: 1893
Name: Willie Groves
Position: Forward
From: West Bromwich Albion
To: Aston Villa
Fee: £105

FIRST FIVE-FIGURE TRANSFER: 1928
Name: David Jack
Position: Forward
From: Bolton Wanderers
To: Arsenal
Fee: £10,000

FIRST SIX-FIGURE TRANSFER: 1961
Name: Luis Suarez Miramontes
Position: Midfielder
From: Barcelona
To: Inter Milan
Fee: £142,000

FIRST EVER £1 MILLIC + TRANSFER: 1975
Name: Guiseppe Savo
Position: Forward
From: Bologna
To: Napoli
Fee: £1.2 million

BUYS

Football transfer fees have gone through the roof in recent years. Teams across the globe have been paying whatever it takes to get the best players. But which are the world's most expensive deals? Here we take a look at the priciest players and some other interesting transfer facts.

4. JOAO FELIX

FROM: BENFICA
TO: ATLETICO MADRID
WHEN: 2019

FEE £113.4 MILLION

Felix is the man Atletico hope will be the long-term replacement for Griezmann. The Portuguese star has made a bright start in Spain and there is plenty more to come.

3. KYLIAN MBAPPE

FROM: AS MONACO
TO: PSG
WHEN: 2018

FEE £121.5 MILLION

Mbappe hasn't looked back since making the switch from Monaco after an initial loan move. The World Cup winner has already won three Ligue 1 titles and scored 90 goals for PSG.

1. NEYMAR

FROM: BARCELONA
TO: PSG
WHEN: 2017

FEE £199.8 MILLION

Neymar's world-record price tag hasn't distracted him as he's continued scoring goals and showboating in equal measure. The magical Brazilian has added three Ligue 1 titles to his impressive trophy cabinet.

2. PHILIPPE COUTINHO

FROM: LIVERPOOL
TO: BARCELONA
WHEN: 2018

FEE £130.5 MILLION

Coutinho left Liverpool in January 2018 but his move hasn't gone to plan so far. He has struggled to impress Barcelona fans and was sent to Bayern Munich on loan for the 2019/20 season.

TOP-10 PRICIEST PLAYERS

(COMBINED TRANSFER FEES)

1. NEYMAR
Combined fees: £279.18 million

2. CRISTIANO RONALDO
Combined fees: £207 million

3. ANGEL DI MARIA
Combined fees: £152.19 million

4. ZLATAN IBRAHIMOVIC
Combined fees: £152.19 million

5. PHILIPPE COUTINHO
Combined fees: £145.62 million

6. GONZALO HIGUAIN
Combined fees: £143.1 million

7. JAMES RODRIGUEZ
Combined fees: £126.57 million

8. OUSMANE DEMBELE
Combined fees: £126 million

9. ROMELU LUKAKU
Combined fees: £124.7 million

10. EDEN HAZARD
Combined fees: £121.5 million

FIRST EVER £10 MILLION + TRANSFER: 1992
Name: Jean-Pierre Papin
Position: Forward
From: Marseille
To: AC Milan
Fee: £10 million

FIRST EVER £100 MILLION + TRANSFER: 2017
Name: Neymar
Position: Forward
From: Barcelona
To: PSG
Fee: £199.8 million

TOM OGDEN

BLOSSOMS

Blossoms stormed the UK charts in 2016 when their self-titled debut album reached number 1.

The band have since toured around the world, played Glastonbury Festival, and topped the charts again with their 2020 album 'Foolish Loving Spaces'.

Lead singer Tom Ogden was born into a fanatical Manchester City family and has supported them through good times and bad.

Tom spoke to Shoot about his City memories, Sergio Aguero's title-winning goal and how Noel Gallagher introduced him to Pep Guardiola.

What are your earliest memories of supporting City?

"The 1998/99 Division 2 play-off winning final season. I remember watching that game at my nana's house with my flag and kit on. The drama of that game was an early sign of what it is like to be a City fan. I became obsessed from that point and went to my first game at Maine Road a few months later. We beat Burnley 5-0 in the League Cup."

Who were your favourite City players growing up?

"Paul Dickov is one. I used to write his name on my shirt in marker pen. Shaun Goater, Mark Kennedy and Kevin Horlock are others. A couple of seasons after that we had Ali Bernarbia who was also a good player and one I liked watching."

What's it been like seeing the club transform into one of the best in Europe?

"I've followed it all the way. We had some good players in the past but I feel the turning point was when we signed Robinho. We were still average but when we got Roberto Mancini as manager and more world-class players things started to change. As a City fan I feel it could end at any time so I just have to enjoy it while it lasts."

Can you tell us how Man City gave Blossoms a big break in 2013?

"Our friend had a few contacts at City and he managed to get us on the City Square Stage pre-match. This was before we were established so it was great to play on a big stage. It was bigger than anything we had done at the time and as a fan I have fond memories of it. We then got to go back and play on derby day plus have supported the Stone Roses at the Etihad. The club have stuck with us and we have a real connection with them. We only have to message them and they sort us out for tickets now which is a nice added bonus."

You've been on the Premier League Show, Soccer AM and interviewed City players. What's that been like for you?

"Those experiences have been really surreal and have given me a lot of great memories. When Phil Foden becomes an England player and I have kids I'll definitely be telling them about the time I interviewed him. It's great to go on these shows, share my passion and meet City players like Phil and Kyle Walker. It's weird because these are not normal things that happen to fans who have a season ticket."

Who's your favourite current player and why?

"Kevin de Bruyne. My favourite players have always been ones who can just pick a pass that nobody else can even see. He reminds me a little bit of Zinedine Zidane in that he makes the game look so easy and effortless."

Favourite moment as a City fan?

"Sergio Aguero's Premier League winning title goal in 2012. There's been some amazing moments as a City fan but nothing will ever compare to that again in my life! I was there with Joe from the band as we had season tickets. I've done a lot of great things in music but none of that comes close to how I felt in the stadium during the last five minutes of that game. We ran on the pitch at the end to celebrate. To snatch the title away from (Manchester) United just put the cherry on top."

Your musical hero Noel Gallagher is also a City fan. Do you speak to him about football?

"We speak about City quite a bit when we see each other. We met through music and when we supported him on tour it was the stuff of dreams for me. The City connection has added to it as we have another thing in common. I have seen him at matches a few times. He has been on the same journey with City I have."

Is it right he introduced you to Pep Guardiola?

"That happened after the Manchester Arena had just reopened. We were performing and our dressing room was next to Noel's. We were talking about City and he said 'Pep is coming down in a bit, I'll come and get you when he is here'. Noel was true to his word. He grabbed me and I was standing there in awe of both of them."

It must be great that your bandmate Joe is also a City fan?

"Our relationship before the band was always music and City. We had season tickets together and have been friends for a very long time. It's also great to have someone else who wants to watch the matches when we're on tour as well."

IN FOCUS

Favourite shirt: 2009/10 home shirt. Very plain but I liked it.

Favourite goal: Aguero's in 2012 vs QPR and Vincent Kompany's vs Leicester in 2019. Both title-winning goals.

Dream signing: Lionel Messi. Obvious but he's the greatest of all time.

Away ground: Not been to too many but I like going to Wigan. It's very old school there.

Ultimate City band: Ederson (drums), Mario Balotelli (frontman), David Silva (guitar), Kevin de Bruyne (keyboards), Paul Dickov (bass).

GUESS THE GAFFER

Gaffer 1

CLUE 1: Managed three different Premier League clubs.

CLUE 2: Won the Champions League as manager with two different clubs.

CLUE 3: Once called himself 'The Special One'.

Jose Mourinho (Tottenham)

Gaffer 2

CLUE 1: Used to be a goalkeeper in his playing days.

CLUE 2: Won the Championship title in his first managerial season in England.

CLUE 3: Is known for having a great beard.

Nuno Espírito Santo

Gaffer 3

CLUE 1: Won seven trophies as a manager in Scotland.

CLUE 2: Managed Liverpool before Jurgen Klopp.

CLUE 3: Born in Northern Ireland.

Brendan Rogers (Leicester)

Gaffer 4

CLUE 1: Three-time Premier League winner as a player.

CLUE 2: Played 106 matches for England between 1999-2014.

CLUE 3: Manages the club where he is the all-time record goalscorer

Frank Lampard (Chelsea)

CLUE 1: Helped his country finish third in the 1998 World Cup.

CLUE 2: Played for and managed West Ham in the Premier League.

CLUE 3: Managed his country at two European Championship tournaments.

CLUE 1: Spent 26 years playing for his boyhood club.

CLUE 2: Finished his playing career in Los Angeles.

CLUE 3: Started his career as a manager in Scotland.

Slaven Bilic (West Brom)

Steven Gerrard (Rangers)

CLUE 1: Won the Champions League as a player and manager.

CLUE 2: One of four Premier League winning Italian managers.

CLUE 3: Returned to manage in England in 2019.

CLUE 1: Played for both Real Madrid and Barcelona.

CLUE 2: Won nine trophies as Barcelona manager.

CLUE 3: Is now the head coach for his country.

Luis Enrique (Barcelona)

Carlo Ancelotti (Everton)

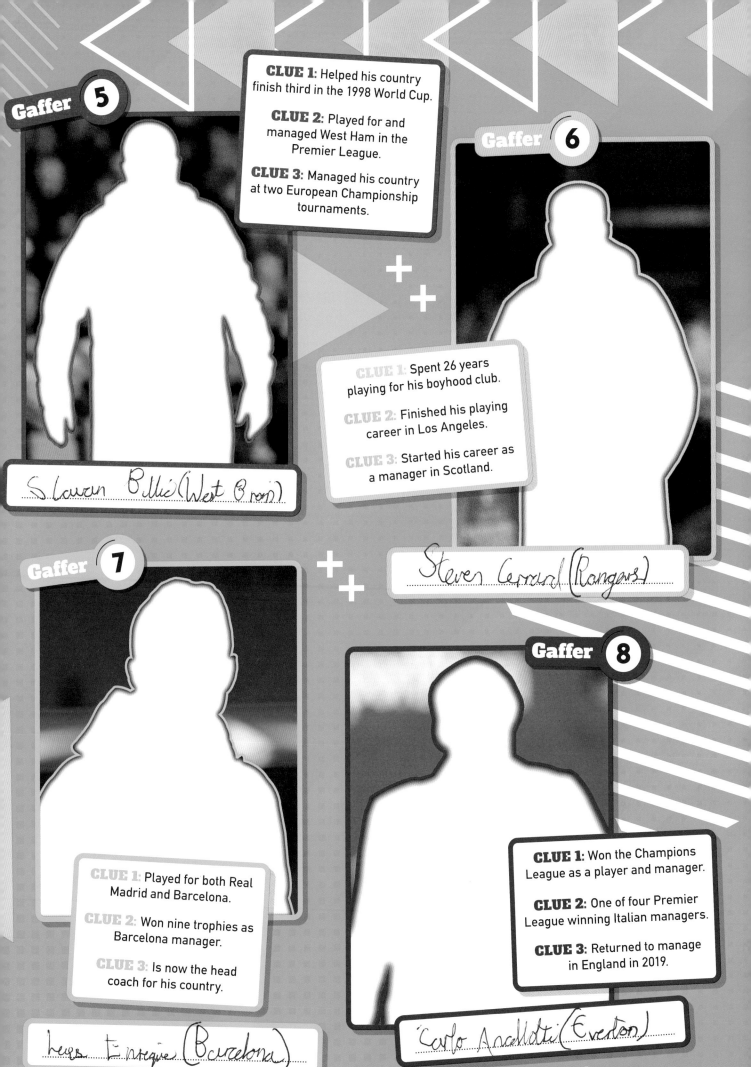

Brendan Rodgers has transformed Leicester City into one of the Premier League's most exciting teams.

The Foxes' fast, free-flowing football sees them challenging the country's biggest clubs at the top end of the Premier League.

Harvey Barnes is one player who has visibly benefitted since Rodgers took charge in February 2019.

Since then the winger has become a regular in the starting XI, scored his first Premier League goals and has been tipped to play for England.

Harvey spoke to Shoot about his progress under Rodgers, targeting an England call-up and how his dad helped his career.

Q: What are your earliest footballing memories?

"When I was really young I caught the last few games my dad played in at the end of his career. I also remember playing for my sides in the local Countesthorpe area. I used to play for the year above but I wasn't allowed to move up with them when we went to 11-a-side. That's when Leicester contacted me and I went to the academy. I was actually unsure about going at the time because I just wanted to play with my friends at that age."

FACT FILE

POSITION: MIDFIELDER / WINGER
HEIGHT: 1.82M (6FT)
BIRTH DATE: DECEMBER 9, 1997
BIRTH PLACE: BURNLEY

HARVEY BARNES

Q: How much has Brendan Rodgers helped you progress as a player?

"When you see him talk you can hear how much he enjoys working with young players. He's brought a new energy to the team and the club. The style of football has been really exciting and we've been scoring a lot of goals. It's great as an attacking player to be involved in. For me it's been great working with a manager who wants to improve individual parts of my game. He's told me to focus on the things that I'm good at. He has had me working on my forward runs and, importantly, getting me to focus on getting in goalscoring positions. It's my job to score goals, create chances and he's helped me with focusing on that."

Q: What was it like to make your Leicester debut in the Champions League against Porto?

"I hadn't really been involved with the first-team much up to that point. I'd trained a few times but didn't know everyone that well so it was nervy. It was great to fly over with the team and have that experience. The game didn't go well for the team (5-0 defeat) but, for me, I had my mum and dad there and it was brilliant. Because we were losing it took the pressure off a lot so I felt I could just go out there and enjoy myself. The whole experience of playing in the Champions League and connecting more with the first-team was really good for me."

Q: Your dad, Paul, was an ex-player. How much of an influence has he had on your career?

"I think he's had a massive influence. For him to have had the football career he had has really helped me. He has a lot of stories he has shared with me plus advice on how to deal with things that happen on and off the pitch. He also helped me with my loan moves. He played first-team at a young age so knew how much it would help and develop me as a player."

Q: Who were your idols growing up?

"As a kid I watched the Manchester United team with Wayne Rooney and Cristiano Ronaldo in a lot. They were two of the best in the Premier League at that time. Watching Ronaldo play, develop and the impact he had on the Premier League was fascinating. I tried to learn and add bits of their game to mine growing up. They obviously did that at the top, top level and that's where every player aims to get to."

Q: How did your loan moves to MK Dons, Barnsley and West Brom help you?

"Making that step from Under-23s to first-team at Premier League level is difficult. At 19, I probably wasn't good enough for Leicester but had outgrown youth football so it was a good step to make. MK Dons was my first loan. I played every week and they played really good football so it was perfect. I then went to Barnsley and West Brom and made a step up each time. I'm lucky that all my loans were successful because that isn't always the case. They set me up and made me ready for when I came back to Leicester."

Q: How does it feel to be regularly playing in the Premier League?

"I am living every kid's dream but I don't really think about what I'm doing because I go from one match or training session to the next. That happens more at the end of the season. There's a lot of pressure playing in the Premier League. I know if I don't perform to the top of my game every day then someone else will come and take my place. That is what I focus on more than thinking about being a Premier League footballer."

Q: Talk us through the Premier League Goal of the Month you scored against Sheffield United in the 2019/20 season...

"The connection was so sweet I thought that even if it was close to the goalkeeper that it had a good chance. It was just one of those where as soon as I hit it I just knew it was going in. It also turned out to be the winning goal which made it extra sweet."

Q: Do you have an eye on an England call-up and making the squad for Euro 2021?

"For myself and all English players it's the dream to represent England, especially at a major tournament. I've been playing well but I think there's still a lot more to come. I just need to keep making sure that my club performances are as high as I can get them to give myself the best opportunity. There's a lot of quality in the squad so it's never going to be easy to get in. But with the Euros now in 2021 I have another year to prove myself and show what I can do."

Q: What advice would you give to any reader who dreams of becoming a footballer?

"Enjoy your football. Always have a football at your feet, practice with your friends and build on your game. You can learn a lot by yourself when you are young by playing as much as you can. If you are playing a lot and enjoying it then you will improve."

IN FOCUS

Day off activity: I like playing golf
Most played artist on your playlist: Drake
Favourite boxset: Money Heist
Funniest teammate: Hamza Choudhury
Superhero power: Power to fly

FIND THE ▶▶▶ ▷▷▷
FULL-BACK

Ten Premier League full-backs are hiding in this wordsearch. Can you find all of them?

Robertson

✓ Bertrand

✓ Davies

✓ Digne

✓ Doherty

✓ Walker

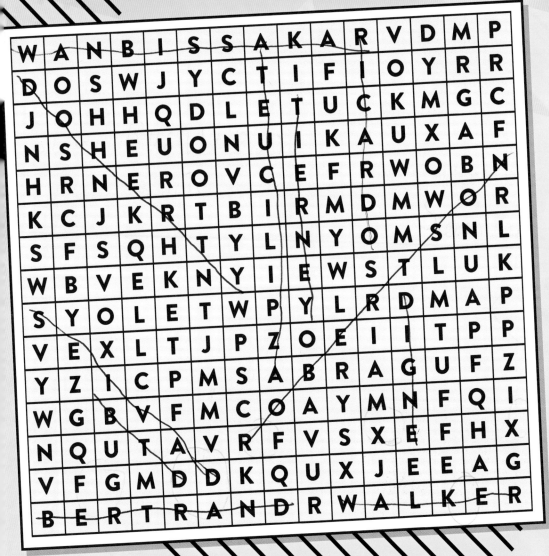

```
W A N B I S S A K A R V D M P
D O S W J Y C T I F I O Y R R
J O H H Q D L E T U C K M G C
N S H E U O N U I K A U X A F
H R N E R O V C E F R W O B N
K C J K R T B I R M D M W O R
S F S Q H T Y L N Y O M S N L
W B V E K N Y I E W S T L U K
S Y O L E T W P Y L R D M A P
V E X L T J P Z O E I L T P P
Y Z I C P M S A B R A G U F Z
W G B V F M C O A Y M N F Q I
N Q U T A V R F V S X E F H X
V F G M D D D K Q U X J E E A G
B E R T R A N D R W A L K E R
```

✓ Ricardo

✓ Azpilicueta

✓ Tierney

✓ Wan-Bissaka

TARGET TEN

Look closely at the two sets of match images below. There are actually 10 differences from picture A to picture B. Can you spot all of them?

PICTURE A

PICTURE B

SHOOT'S SUPER QUIZ

SECOND HALF

You've had your half-time drink and team talk. Now it's time for the second half of our ultimate quiz. Remember, you get one point for each correct answer. Good luck!

21 Which number does Trent Alexander-Arnold wear at Liverpool?

66

22 Southampton play their home games at which stadium?

St Marys

23 What is the nickname of Cardiff City?

The blue birds

24 How many times has Lionel Messi won the Champions League?

4

25 Zlatan Ibrahimovic returned to which Italian club in December 2019?

AC Milan

26 Which country knocked England out of the 2019 Women's World Cup?

USA

27 In what year did the new Wembley Stadium open – 2005, 2007, 2009?

2007

28 Which former Manchester United and Everton player will leave his role as England women's manager in 2021?

Jamie Carragher

29

Name this player who had the most assists in the 2019/20 Premier League season…

KDB

30

Cristiano Ronaldo scored 28, 32 or 35 goals in his first season playing for Juventus?

32

31

Newcastle forward Miguel Almiron is from which country?

Paraguay

32

True or false? Rangers have a bigger stadium than Celtic?

True

33

Which Chelsea player is nicknamed Dave?

Cesar Azpilicueta

34

Name the missing World Cup winning country – Brazil, Germany, Uruguay, Italy, France, England, Spain and…

Argentina West Germany

35

V's 0

Which club set a Premier League away record with a 9-0 win in October 2019?

Leicester

36

What was the record FA Cup final score between Man City and Watford in 2019?

6 - 0

37

Which major European club plays at Parc de Princes?

PSG

38

I'm Manchester United's latest star…..
Bruno Fernandes

ruo Fnardes

39

Benfica and Sporting CP play in which Portuguese city?

Lisbon

40

Which bird of prey is on Crystal Palace's badge?

Eagle

ANSWERS ON PAGE 77

BELIEVE IT
OR NOT

Football is a funny old game sometimes. Here's a selection of weird and wonderful facts. Believe it or not, they are all true...

AC Milan legend Alessandro Nesta once missed a month after injuring himself playing the PlayStation. He had an all-night gaming session which led to him requiring thumb surgery. We just hope he finished the mission first.

No German team has ever broken the world transfer record but Scottish side Falkirk have. They paid a massive £5,000 for Syd Puddefoot in 1922. That is just £199.995 million less than Neymar cost PSG in 2018. How times have changed.

Netherlands and Arsenal legend Dennis Bergkamp was nicknamed the 'Non-flying Dutchman'. A fear of flying meant he'd miss matches or even drive across Europe. Imagine how many service stations he's visited.

Juan Mata and Fernando Torres once held the Champions League, Europa League, World Cup and European Championship all at the same time. The Spaniards won the Europa League in 2013 while the other three medals came in 2010 and 2012. Impressive!

Sunderland inserted a very unusual contract clause when they signed Stefan Schwarz from Valencia in 1999. The deal prevented the Swedish midfielder from going into space. He didn't travel the solar system but did help the Black Cats reach the dizzy heights of seventh in his first two seasons.

Chelsea striker Olivier Giroud was the voice of the Green Goblin in the French edition of Spider-man: Into the Spider-Verse. We can only assume it ends with a penalty shootout to decide the fate of the universe.

All of the last four goalkeepers to lose World Cup finals played for AS Monaco at the time. We think the French side might have a hard time getting a 'keeper for the 2022/23 season.

When Arsenal played Dynamo Moscow in 1945, the fog was so bad that both sides sneaked players onto the pitch. It was so thick the referee didn't notice that Dynamo had 15 players on at one time!

Mexican striker Hugo Sánchez scored 38 goals in the 1989/90 season for Real Madrid. What was unusual was that all of them were first time finishes. A real fox in the box.

Switzerland were knocked out of the 2006 World Cup despite not conceding a single goal. They lost on penalties to Ukraine after a 0-0 draw in the last-16. Maybe attack would have been the best form of defence after all.

Liverpool star James Milner won the PFA Young Player of the Year EIGHT years after making his Premier League debut in 2002. He must have found the mythical Fountain of Youth.

If you looked up to space at the right time you might have seen Arsene Wenger. That's because the former Arsenal manager actually has an asteroid named after him.

CAPTION THIS

Football is a funny old game. The Shoot team have forgotten to add the captions to these seven images. Can you help us by filling in the blanks with clever captions? Use your imagination. There are no right or wrong answers.

Caption this...

" Wooooooooo ohooooooo "

Caption this... Ah my daily run

"

"

Caption this... oh no I've got hair lice

"

"

Caption this... Ready or not here

" I come "

Caption this...

" EXHAUSTEO "

Caption this... Two down Injured

"

"

Caption this...

" I'm flying "

ADDED TIME

There's no better feeling in football than scoring in added time. That feeling is even sweeter if that last gasp goal bags your team points. Can you name these 2019/20 Premier League added-time superheroes?

MATCH 1 — LIVERPOOL vs Everton

Goalscorer:
....

MATCH 2 — NEWCASTLE vs Chelsea

Goalscorer:
....

MATCH 3 — Burnley vs MAN UNITED

Goalscorer:
....

MATCH **4** **LEICESTER vs Watford**

Goalscorer:
....

MATCH **5** **Brighton vs SOUTHAMTON**

Goalscorer:
....

MATCH **6** **SHEFF UTD vs Man United**

Goalscorer:
....

ANSWERS ON PAGE 77

ANSWERS

8-9 NAME THAT PLAYER

1. Patrick van Aanholt
2. Raheem Sterling
3. Antonio Rudiger
4. Andrew Robertson
5. Eric Dier
6. Anthony Martial
7. Theo Walcott
8. Nicolas Pepe
9. Nathan Redmond
10. Ashley Barnes

14-15 GUESS THAT GROUND

1. Loftus Road
2. Elland Road
3. St James' Park
4. Villa Park
5. Etihad Stadium
6. Ewood Park
7. Anfield
8. Fratton Park
9. Tottenham Hotspur Stadium
10. Stadium of Light

16-17 SPOT THE BALL

GAME 1: C   GAME 2: C
GAME 3: A   GAME 4: D

18-19 THE AGE GAME

Lionel Messi - 1987

Cristiano Ronaldo - 1985

Jack Grealish – 1995

Son Heung-min – 1992

Paul Pogba – 1993

Zlatan Imbrahimovic – 1981

Billy Gilmour – 2001

Kylian Mbappe – 1998

Eden Hazard – 1991

Alphonso Davies – 2000

26-27 SPOT THE STARS

30-31 SALAH, FIRMINO OR MANE?

1. Salah	5. Mane	9. Firmino	13. Salah
2. Mane	6. Salah	10. Salah	14. Mane
3. Firmino	7. Firmino	11. Mane	15. Salah
4. Firmino	8. Mane	12. Firmino	

32-33 SHOOT'S SUPER QUIZ - 1ST HALF

1. Inter Miami
2. Senegal
3. Serge Gnabry
4. Swansea City
5. Michael O'Neill
6. Loftus Road
7. Borussia Dortmund
8. Steven Bergwijn
9. Gonzalo Higuain
10. Rodri
11. Spain
12. Antoine Griezmann
13. Ipswich Town
14. DC United
15. Watford
16. Kieran Trippier
17. Arsenal
18. Roberto Firmino
19. Bramall Lane (Sheffield United)
20. Scotland

43 KIT SWAP

Odsonne Edouard - Shirt C, Shorts B, Socks D

Kevin De Bruyne - Shirt D, Shorts A, Socks C

Ruben Neves - Shirt B, Shorts D, Socks A

Richarlison - Shirt A, Shorts C, Socks B

60-61 GUESS THE GAFFER

1. Jose Mourinho	5. Slaven Bilic
2. Nuno Espirito Santo	6. Steven Gerrard
3. Brendan Rodgers	7. Luis Enrique
4. Frank Lampard	8. Carlo Ancelotti

65 FIND THE FULL-BACK

W	A	N	B	I	S	S	K	A	R	V	D	M	P
D	O	S	W	J	Y	C	T	I	F	I	O	Y	R	R
J	O	H	H	Q	D	L	E	T	U	C	K	M	G	C
N	S	H	E	U	O	N	U	I	K	A	U	X	A	F
H	R	N	E	R	O	V	C	E	F	R	W	O	B	N
K	C	J	K	R	T	B	I	R	M	D	M	W	O	R
S	F	S	Q	H	T	Y	L	N	Y	O	M	S	N	L
W	B	V	E	K	N	I	E	W	S	T	L	U	K
S	Y	O	L	E	T	W	P	Y	L	R	D	M	A	P
V	E	X	L	T	J	P	Z	O	E	I	I	T	P	P
Y	Z	I	C	P	M	S	A	B	R	A	G	U	F	Z
W	G	B	V	F	M	C	O	A	Y	M	N	F	Q	I
N	Q	U	T	A	V	F	V	S	X	E	F	H	X
V	F	G	M	D	D	K	Q	U	X	J	E	E	A	G
B	E	R	T	R	A	N	D	R	W	A	L	K	E	R

66-67 TARGET TEN

68-69 SHOOT'S SUPER QUIZ - 2ND HALF

21. 66	31. Paraguay
22. St Mary's	32. False
23. Bluebirds	33. Cesar Azpilicueta
24. 4	34. Argentina
25. AC Milan	35. Leicester City
26. United States	36. Man City 6-0 Watford
27. 2007	37. Paris Saint-Germain
28. Phil Neville	38. Bruno Fernandes
29. Kevin De Bruyne	39. Lisbon
30. 28	40. Eagle

74-75 ADDED TIME

1. Georginio Wijnaldum	4. James Maddison
2. Isaac Hayden	5. Nathan Redmond
3. Marcus Rashford	6. Oli McBurnie

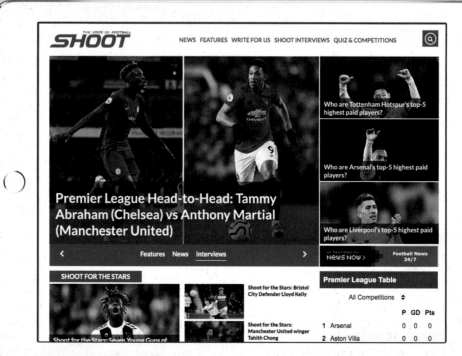
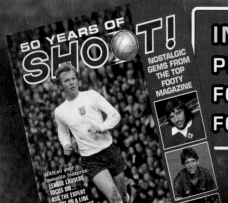